STUDIES IN ENGLISH LITERATURE

Volume LIX

THE

REFLECTOR,

A

QUARTERLY MAGAZINE,

ON SUBJECTS OF PHILOSOPHY, POLITICS, AND THE LIBERAL ARTS.

CONDUCTED BY THE EDITOR OF THE EXAMINER.

Omnis cogitatio motusque animi, aut in consiliis capiendis de rebus honestis et pertinentibus ad bene beateque vivendum, aut in studiis scientiæ cognitionisque, versatur.

CICERO.

VOL. I.

FROM OCTOBER 1810, TO MARCH 1811, INCLUSIVE,

London:

PRINTED AND PUBLISHED BY JOHN HUNT, EXAMINER-OFFICE, BEAUFORT BUILDINGS, STRAND:—SOLD BY J. CARPENTER, OLD BOND-STREET, AND ALL BOOKSELLERS.

1811.

LEIGH HUNT'S *REFLECTOR*

by

KENNETH E. KENDALL
University of Florida

1971
MOUTON
THE HAGUE · PARIS

LIBRARY OF CONGRESS CATALOG CARD NUMBER: 75-129295

Printed in The Netherlands by Mouton & Co., Printers, The Hague.

To My Parents
Vernon and Ruth Kendall

PREFACE

In recent years scholars have given increased attention to biographical and editorial work on Leigh Hunt and his writings. His tremendous output makes a complete edition impractical, and the ephemeral nature of much of his writing makes editorial work necessarily selective. Since Hunt and the periodical are inextricably associated, however, most of the magazines which he edited have received scholarly treatment.

An exception is the *Reflector*, Hunt's first magazine, published in 1811-1812 concurrently with his editorship of the *Examiner*. While it has received some critical prominence and some of its essays have been reprinted and anthologized, no one has yet made a separate study of Hunt's "chronicle for posterity", as he called it in the Prospectus.

This examination of the *Reflector* throws the critical searchlight on that chronicle. The purpose is fourfold: to show something of the mind of the time as revealed in the *Reflector*, to reconsider some of the nearly forgotten writers associated with the magazine, to establish the authorship of some of the anonymous articles, and to evaluate the periodical in terms of its literary and political significance.

The names of Leigh Hunt and Charles Lamb dominate the roster of contributors to the *Reflector*. Indeed, the *Reflector* owes most of its historical and literary merit to those two men, and that merit stems primarily from their imaginative writings in its pages.

Most of the minor contributors – professionals like Dr. John Aikin, George Dyer, and Octavius Gilchrist and talented amateurs like Hunt's personal friends Thomas Barnes, Barron Field,

Thomas Mitchell, and James Scholefield – are remembered today largely because of their association with Hunt and Lamb. Heretofore these minor writers have received little or no biographical or critical attention. Yet all of these writers, and many of the anonymous ones as well, made some contribution to the magazine as a reflector of its times.

Still Leigh Hunt and Charles Lamb remain the stellar attractions of the *Reflector*. And without shading in any way the light which Lamb lent to the magazine, one conclusion becomes increasingly clear from a study of its pages: Hunt himself deserves greater recognition as the magazine's founder, editor, and principal contributor; as one who influenced both Lamb and the familiar essay; as a literary voice for the early reform movement; and as a man of letters at the height of his self-confident power, the center of a coterie, a star with its own satellites – just as he was to become, in a few years, a satellite to a circle of stars brighter than he.

Being contemporary with Wordsworth, Coleridge, Byron, Shelley, and Keats was somewhat of a mixed blessing for Hunt, who will always hold an inferior rank to these men of genius; but in Leigh Hunt, a minor genius of the Romantic period, can be found much that illumines the period, and his magazine reflects considerable light.

Like the *Reflector*, this book has been made possible by "the assistance of various other hands". To Blunden, Landrè, Lucas, and others the obligation is obvious and immeasurable. Special thanks go to the late Dr. Stephen F. Fogle for his generous help and advice; to the librarians of the University of Florida and the University of Iowa; to Dr. E. Ashby Hammond and Dr. Thomas Pyles for their interest and support; and to Dr. Alton C. Morris for his counsel, strength, and wisdom as "guide, philosopher, and friend".

CONTENTS

I

THE NATURE OF THE *REFLECTOR* PERIOD, 1810-1812

In the spring of 1810 John and Leigh Hunt, proprietors of the successful weekly newspaper, the *Examiner*, projected a new quarterly magazine, to be called the *Reflector*, which, they promised, would be an improvement over its contemporaries in the coverage of politics, the fine arts, "and all subjects relative to Wit, Morals, and a true Refinement".[1]

In its four issues and its fifteen months of life, the *Reflector*, published by John and edited by Leigh Hunt, did much to fulfill this promise. In continuing and repeating the political sentiments of the *Examiner*, it reflected the political discontent of the time so thoroughly that politics permeated much of its editor's imaginative writing. It not only reported the current endeavors in art, architecture, and the drama but included the editor's evaluation and personal comments. It reflected some of the literary and social concepts of the Romantic period and, as its greatest claim to immortality, rendered an immeasurable service to literature: in Lamb's critical and early personal essays, in Hunt's poetry and his personal essays, and in the influence of both Lamb and Hunt on the development of the familiar essay. As Hunt wrote in the Prospectus, the *Reflector* was an attempt to portray the mind of the times for its contemporaries and for posterity, and the result was a product, not of an ivory tower, but of the political, journalistic, and literary milieu of the years 1810 to 1812.

[1] Prospectus, p. viii of the bound volumes of the *Reflector*. The separate copy of the Prospectus in the British Museum (823.C.1.52) bears the date "April 1810" and the line "The First Number is in the press, and will appear as soon as possible". (It appeared eight months later, about January 1, 1811.)

A paragraph in the *Examiner* at the end of 1810, copied from the *Stamford News*, concisely describes the turbulent world into which the *Reflector* was born:

State of the nation – Bankruptcies, unprecedented in number, occasioned by a ruined commerce – a depreciated paper currency, and the disappearance of the precious metals – a national expenditure which Mr. Huskisson, the friend of Mr. Pitt, says cannot much longer be supported – an enormous taxation, which Mr. Huskisson says cannot be encreased – an army in Portugal, which everybody says can do no good – an imperfect representation, which the House of Commons say shall not be reformed – his Majesty incapacitated – Mr. Perceval his minister – Mr. Yorke at the head of the Admiralty – and Bonaparte at the head of the French nation – these are a few of "the evils which surround and oppress us." [2]

The long and disappointing war with France was still in progress and was to continue for another five years. Napoleon had a firm grip on the continent, except for parts of the Spanish peninsula where Wellington was having limited success in circumventing his designs. His Continental System was the cause of financial distress in England, and the loss of European markets closed factories and brought lengthened lists of bankruptcies to the columns of the *Examiner*. The effects of the industrial revolution were being felt in the rise in urban population and an enlarged and wealthy middle class – a new feudalism, the factory, had replaced that of the castle. The first census had been taken in 1801 by Lamb's friend, John Rickman, and the first steamboat made its appearance the same year. The need for increased agricultural production to feed the army and the growing population called for larger farms and more enclosures, some two million acres being enclosed between 1790 and 1810. But three years of poor crops depressed the agricultural interests in 1810 and food prices were high. Unemployment was common. Labor-saving machinery was blamed for the unemployment rate and wholesale destruction of machinery, or frame-breaking, resulted in the Luddite Riots.

Some of the blame for conditions could be traced to the revered William Pitt, though probably not to the extent that Leigh Hunt

[2] *Examiner* (1810), p. 824.

insisted.[3] But he did leave the country deeply in debt and involved in the conflict with France. The brief rule of Fox and his cabinet of all talents, which marked the end of forty-three years of Whig administration, managed only one significant reform, the abolition of the slave trade. From 1807 to the late 1820's the Tories were in power, with Spencer Perceval as head of the cabinet through the *Reflector* period, until his assassination in 1812. His cabinet was illiberal in its policies, resisting any change in the status quo – and the Hunts had become increasingly ardent in opposing that status quo. The Whigs were ineffective as an opposition party because they were split into liberal and conservative factions. A small group of reformers, Sir Francis Burdett's Radicals, was progressive and independent of party lines, and Burdett was considered the leader of the Reformists and protector of popular liberties, though his actions were sometimes rash and embarrassing. Under Pitt and the influence of the French Revolution, agitation for reform had almost died out, but in the *Reflector* period this agitation was revived, with the cabinet in opposition to all popular movements. The government in 1810 did not represent the will of the people, and the reformists believed that parliamentary reforms would bring a modification of other social evils. Reform was not to come for another decade, but the name of Leigh Hunt remains associated with early reform efforts through his *Examiner* and *Reflector* articles.

In 1810 George III was still on the throne, but he was already "an old, mad, blind, despised, and dying king", his reign virtually over, as Hunt noted astutely in one of his *Reflector* articles (II, 182). In the Prince of Wales Hunt saw the only hope for the leadership which could result in an alleviation of the political and social conditions, and Hunt directed his advice and admonitions to him. In 1810 there was hope that the Prince, as regent, would appoint a new ministry, but 1811 showed the fruitlessness of these hopes. The Prince was vulgar and virtueless, and the crescendo of criticism which Hunt directed at him was to result in the imprisonment of the Hunts for libel.

[3] *Reflector*, I, 3-5; 453-457. (Subsequent citations to the *Reflector* will be to Volume and page and inserted in the text.)

The rise of a wealthy middle class and the increase in the reading population swelled the number of magazines being published after 1790. In spite of the government's control of the press by means of stamped paper, about forty new magazines appeared in the 1790's and twenty more in the first decade of the new century, though many of them, like the *Reflector*, did not last long. During the second decade of the century about thirty magazines were being published in London alone. Two of the most enduring were the *Gentleman's Magazine*, which had been started in 1731, and the *European Magazine*, in 1782. They contained extracts of books, articles gleaned from other journals, and letters and essays sent in by readers. After the turn of the century, however, these periodicals were publishing more original material, and they tried to be instructive and entertaining. Of the reviews, the *Monthly Review* dates from 1749, but the two most prominent reviews of the *Reflector* period were the *Edinburgh Review* of Francis Jeffrey, founded in 1802, and the *Quarterly*, begun in 1809 by William Gifford.

Politics became more prominent in periodical literature after 1800. William Cobbett's *Weekly Register* voiced the radical opinions outside of parliament. In 1810 Cobbett was sentenced to two years in prison for criticizing the cabinet, but after the close of the war with France in 1815 he continued to press for parliamentary reform. The *Examiner* started in 1808 as an independent newspaper, but its views soon became increasingly reformist; by the time the *Reflector* was inaugurated, Hunt could write that its viewpoint would coincide with that of the *Examiner,* strongly reformist, but independent, because he did not know any politicians personally.

The essay form in 1810 was still much the same as it had been in the eighteenth century, and Hunt acknowledged his indebtedness to Addison and Steele and to the *Connoisseur* in his *Autobiography*. Themes were largely moralistic; the Johnson dictum that essays should "inculcate wisdom and piety" still persisted. Writers sometimes spoke through a persona, often in a letter signed with an apt pseudonym. The character sketch was another favorite device, more often in imitation of La Bruyere than of Theophrastus, and often didactic in nature. The dream or vision was an old form, used by Addison for moral purposes, as was the oriental tale; both were used by Hunt in the *Reflector*. Late in the century essays tended to become more informative, more factual than critical, and some writers attempted to promote public interest in the arts. The essay serial persisted through the eighteenth century, but by 1810 it was weakening;[4] the *Reflector* contained the beginnings of several serials, among them Lamb's "Theatralia, No. 1" and three by Dr. John Aikin. Lamb's only personal essay prior to those in the *Reflector* was one in the *London Magazine* in 1802. Hunt had published several brief descriptive essays in the *Examiner*, but his real beginning in the personal essay was in the *Reflector*. The personal essay prior to the *Reflector* was still largely traditional, but in the *Reflector* Hunt's "A Day by the Fire" shows signs of moving toward the familiar essay.

When the *Reflector* was born, the Romantic Period was already well advanced. The *Lyrical Ballads* had been published for twelve years, and Wordsworth at forty and Coleridge at thirty-eight had their best work behind them. Blake at fifty-three had produced the bulk of his poems and engravings and was still relatively unknown outside a select circle of friends, though his paintings had received some notoriety in two *Examiner* articles by Robert Hunt.[5] Byron at twenty-three was on the grand tour; he had taken his seat in the House of Lords, had published *English Bards and Scotch Reviewers*, and had written the first canto of *Childe Harold*. Henry Crabb Robinson was about to begin his famous diary, and Thomas Moore was publishing his *Irish Melodies*. Shelley was only eighteen and a student at Oxford; Keats at sixteen was still in the Clarke school at Enfield. Charles Lamb was thirty-five, an old employee at East India House and author, with his sister, of *Tales from Shakespeare*. Leigh Hunt was twenty-six, one of the younger Romantics who was to outlive all

[4] Melvin R. Watson, *Magazine Serials and the Essay Tradition, 1746-1820* (Baton Rouge, 1956), p. 68.

[5] "Blake's Edition of Blair's Grave" in the *Examiner* (August 7, 1808), pp. 509-510 and "Mr. Blake's Exhibition" (September 17, 1809), p. 605.

of them, a prominent newspaper editor, the center of a coterie, and already a controversial figure.

Against this background of war, depression, discontent, agitation, social change, and transition, the Hunts decided to show the world that they could put out a better magazine than any then in existence. To say that they succeeded in this competitive design would be presumptuous in the light of its short life, even though failure in its purpose did not cause its demise. The *Reflector* recorded the spirit of the times, and in the judgment of the posterity for which it was a chronicle, its continuing importance lies in the literary contributions of Charles Lamb and of its editor, Leigh Hunt.

II

LEIGH HUNT AND THE *REFLECTOR*

Leigh Hunt's connection with the *Reflector* was threefold: as part owner, as editor, and as principal contributor. He and his brother owned both the *Examiner* and the *Reflector* and Leigh was editor of both periodicals. Hunt's contributions to the new magazine included political and theatrical criticism, translations, poetry, satire, and the personal essay. His need for another outlet for his literary works was a motive for inaugurating the *Reflector*.

Hunt's literary career had been launched unwisely and too well by his father with *Juvenilia* (1801), which went to five editions, four English and one American, by 1804. Born in 1784 and educated at Christ's Hospital from 1791 to 1799, Hunt was younger than Charles Lamb and Thomas Mitchell and older than Thomas Barnes and James Scholefield, the other old Bluecoat boys who wrote for the *Reflector*. While supporting himself by working as a clerk in the War Office, Hunt wrote theatrical reviews for his brother's papers, the *News* and the *Statesman,* establishing what was at that time a new and unusual policy of honest, unbiased reporting and recording a wealth of information on the actors and the acting style of the period. Some of his reviews were published in book form early in 1808.[1] *Classic Tales* by Hunt and Reynell appeared from 1806 to 1808. From 1808 to 1821 Hunt was editor of the *Examiner*, doing the principal articles entitled "The Political Examiner" and the "Theatrical

[1] *Critical Essays on the Performers of the London Theatres*, including general observations on the practise and genius of the Stage: by the author of the Theatrical Criticism in the weekly paper called the News. John Hunt, 1807 (dated 1807, but published in 1808).

Examiner" as well as occasional poems and sketches, all signed with his familiar "indicator" or pointing finger.

In the *Reflector* period Hunt was at the height of his creative power, possessed of a self-confident courage that was to be dampened somewhat by his prison term for libel from 1813 to 1815. His editorship of the *Examiner* made him an influential public figure, one whose independence brought him the respect of the public and the animosity of politicians, theatre managers, and some of the actors. While the *Examiner* and its editor disclaimed any connection with a party ("Party is the madness of the many for the gain of the few" was their motto), they were aligned with the reformists, who had no party *per se*, in their opposition to both Whigs and conservatives and their support of reform in parliament at every opportunity. Their opposition to the government and their sometimes reckless statements brought the Hunt brothers four expensive experiences with *ex officio* information for libel and two-year prison terms for their libel against the Prince Regent.

The *Examiner* was doing well enough by the end of its first year – circulation was 2,200 copies per week – for Hunt, somewhat embarrassed by his dual role of servant and critic of the government, to leave his War Office job and to marry Marianne Hunter the following July 3, 1809. For two years they lived in Beckenham, Kent, ten miles from the *Examiner* office in the Strand; in 1811 they moved to Hampstead. The year 1810 was a busy and eventful one for Hunt. His father, Isaac Hunt, died in January. In April a "Memoir of Mr. James Henry Leigh Hunt, Written by Himself (With a Portrait)" appeared in the *Monthly Mirror*, published by his friend Thomas Hill. The portrait, painted by Jackson and engraved by Freeman, shows Hunt to be the serious and contemplative person of his later portraits but, unlike them, indolent and heavy. In September the first of his nine children was born. This was Thornton Leigh Hunt, who was to emulate his father by becoming a writer, to become Lamb's "favorite child",[2] and to be remembered as much for breaking up

[2] "To T.L.H." in the *Examiner* (January 1, 1815), p. 9, signed "C.L.".

Leigh Hunt in 1810

(Painting by Jackson, engraving by Freeman,
Published in "Monthly Mirror" for April, 1810)
(Copyright, National Portrait Gallery)

the home of his friend and business partner, George Henry Lewes, as for editing his father's *Poetical Works* (1860) and *Correspondence* (1862). On October 13 Hunt became an honorary member of a "Philosophical Society" [3] and on October 18 he observed his twenty-sixth birthday.

Hunt spent his time reading, writing, attending plays, and enjoying his friends. His social life was always active, at his home, at the homes of friends, and at the Sydenham Tusculum of Thomas Hill. Politics, literature, and the fine arts all had their moments in discussion and debate – the crucible of free expression in which Hunt's ideas could be tested for his columns in the *Examiner*. Many of his companions at this time were his old Christ's Hospital friends, Barnes, Scholefield, and Mitchell; others included Theodore Hook, Mathews the actor, the Smith brothers, Barron Field of the *Times*, Godwin, Fuseli, West, Kinnaird. As Lamb was to observe, friendships formed at Christ's Hospital were lasting ones, and, like Lamb, Hunt had a talent for friendship. Hunt himself wrote, "Friendship was a romantic passion with me",[4] and "I call friendship the most spiritual of the affections".[5] A less admirable characteristic was Hunt's naïveté in matters of money, a trait which he blamed partly on having attended the grammar school at Christ's Hospital rather than the mathematical or navigation school, but it was more a matter of responsibility and common sense than an ability to compute. He was an inveterate borrower, and in September of 1810 he had notes from Barron Field and Thomas Mitchell mentioning sums they had advanced to him.[6] He had begun a life of borrowing, of debts, and of shortages of money. Hunt had a generous nature and would share what he had with his friends, except that he rarely had any money to lend; he felt that anyone who had money should share it. Strictly speaking, Hunt's primary interest was not journal-

[3] Louis Landré, *Leigh Hunt (1784-1859). Contribution à l'histoire du romantisme anglais*, 2 vols. (Paris, 1936), I, 58.

[4] *Leigh Hunt's Autobiography, The Earliest Sketches*, ed. Stephen F. Fogle (Gainesville, Florida, 1959), p. xiii.

[5] *The Autobiography of Leigh Hunt*, ed. J. E. Morpurgo (London, 1949), p. 83.

[6] Landré, I, 63.

ism but *belles lettres* – reading, translating, composing – "I was almost always absorbed in my books and verses", he wrote in his *Autobiography*,[7] and he usually had difficulty getting to the task of his weekly columns. Late in 1810 he prepared a plan for *The Planet of the Poets* in three cantos, but this seems to have been abandoned in favor of *The Feast of the Poets*, which he published a year or so later in the *Reflector*. The weekly newspaper was not a suitable medium for printing poems and essays, though he did insert an occasional sketch or poem in its columns. His literary tendencies could not be suppressed; he filled his columns with quotations and allusions in several languages. He was almost too "literary" for a newspaperman, but this trait may have accounted for some of the *Examiner's* appeal among the educated classes.

Such was the situation in 1810 when John Hunt "projected a quarterly magazine of literature and politics, entitled the *Reflector*, which I edited".[8] John was the business man of the pair and he must have "projected" the quarterly in expectations of its financial returns and greater utilization of his plant and equipment. Perhaps the situation seemed to call for a new periodical to answer the needs of Leigh Hunt even more than the public need for another magazine, although the increase in the number of periodicals during the first three decades of the nineteenth century reflected the expanded reading public and a greater demand for reading material. Hunt had many friends ready and willing to write for him, for they could all use the *Reflector*'s liberal fees even though writing was a sideline for some of them. And Hunt knew enough professional writers who could fill pages for him, if need be: Octavius Gilchrist, Dr. John Aikin, and George Dyer, for example. Charles Lamb was to come later, an unexpected bonus for Hunt – and posterity. Primarily, however, Hunt could use an outlet for such of his own literary work as was unsuitable for the *Examiner*. Then too a new literary magazine could reinforce the political attitudes of the *Examiner*, attracting the reformists and making new converts to reform with its literary approach.

7 P. 223.
8 *Autobiography*, p. 214.

For the title of their new magazine the Hunts chose the *Reflector*, appropriate because of its double meaning of a mirror and a thinker. "Thinking man" and "thinking nation" were favorite topics and expressions with Hunt in the *Examiner* and in the *Reflector*.[9] A Prospectus dated in April was circulated and later printed in the bound volumes as a preface, but extant correspondence from the period is silent about any details of the projected publication until December; in fact, there is surprisingly little mention of the *Reflector* at all. The first issue came out late in December or early January; Landrè dates it about January 1, 1811.[10] Dating the first volume, which contains the first two issues, "From October 1810, to March 1811, inclusive" has given the erroneous impression that the first issue came out in October and is dated October, but the dates indicate the coverage of events in the retrospect or chronicle articles. The irregularity of publication made it difficult to break the chronicles into neat quarterly packages; the second Retrospect, for example, covers six months' events from December to mid-June 1811. The last paragraph of the first "Retrospect of Public Affairs" begins with the line, "Such is the general state of affairs, abroad and at home, in this concluding month of the year 1810" (I, 242). Writing to Marianne on a Saturday evening in December 1810, Hunt says that "the Reflector will not be out till next week".[11]

The new magazine does not seem to have caused a stir in the literary world, judging from the paucity of comment in the press. It was noticed in various magazines under their listings of "New Publications", but only the *Satirist* made critical comment, and that as usual was caustic. The November 30, 1810, issue of the *Belfast Monthly Magazine* noted "The Reflector, No. 1, a quarterly Magazine, on Subjects of Philosophy, Politics, and the Liberal Arts, conducted by the Editor of the Examiner, 5s", copying its description from the title page.[12] The February 1811 issue of the *Edinburgh Review* listed "The Reflector (to be con-

[9] Preface to the 1809 *Examiner*; the *Reflector*, I, 1-16; II, 11, 206, 428.

[10] Landré, II, 486.

[11] Luther A. Brewer, *My Leigh Hunt Library – The Holograph Letters* (Iowa City, 1938), p. 51.

[12] *Belfast Monthly Magazine*, V (November 30, 1810), 385.

tinued Quarterly). No. I, 6s".[13] Since magazines of the day rarely, if ever, appeared on their printed dates (The August 1811 *Quarterly Review*, for instance, came out in October),[14] the notice in the Belfast magazine only shows that the *Monthly* itself was two or three months late. The *Belfast* seems to have erred in the matter of price, as it lists the first issue for five shillings, the second for six, and the third for sixpence, while the *Edinburgh Review* consistently lists six shillings, the usual price for a magazine of this size and format. The *Quarterly Review* did not notice the new magazine at all, even under its listing of new publications. The *Examiner*, strangely, is completely silent about its sister publication, the only mention of it being in a letter to the editor early in January 1811 about the Prospectus. Henry Crabb Robinson read the first issue on May 15.[15] The *Satirist* for February 1, 1811, enjoyed making fun of Hunt, "the literary *Janus* whose *Examiner* applies to our superiors, and whose *Reflector* is to be applied to our *posteriors*, for such is the idea suggested by his very modest prospectus . . . a work designed for posterity, and therefore not likely to be read by the existing generation".[16] The *Satirist* article, signed "Echo", concentrates on Hunt's prefatory remarks to his translation of "Atys the Enthusiast".

The *Reflector,* printed and published "by John Hunt, Examiner-Office, Beaufort Buildings, Strand", used the same type, the same rough paper and brown ink as the *Examiner*. The issues were planned for about 240 pages each, or fifteen sheets (the third issue was only fourteen sheets) with a light olive green wrapper or cover. Like the *Edinburgh Review* and the *Quarterly* and other magazines of its size, its six-shilling price made it as expensive as a book. After the *Reflector* discontinued in 1812, the sheets were bound into two volumes octavo in half calf and in half green morocco with the Prospectus and, in some volumes, a postscript

[13] *Edinburgh Review*, XVII (February 1811), 498.

[14] Hill Shine and Helen Chadwick Shine, *The Quarterly Review under Gifford* (Chapel Hill, 1949), p. 24.

[15] *The Works of Charles and Mary Lamb*, ed. E. V. Lucas (London, 1903), I, 405.

[16] *The Satirist or Monthly Meteor*, VIII (February 1, 1811), 123.

about its discontinuance. The two different printings of the title page indicate that some of the bound copies were put out in the first half of 1812, when the *Examiner* was located in the Strand, and the rest after the week of August 23, 1812, during which the *Examiner* moved to 21 Maiden Lane, Covent Garden. The earlier binding of the *Reflector* has the following title page, which follows that of the original individual issues:

The Reflector, / A / Quarterly Magazine, / on Subjects of Philosophy, Politics, and the / Liberal Arts./ (Printer's rule) Conducted by the Editor in The Examiner./ (Printer's rule) Omnis cogitatio motusque animi, aut in consiliis capiendis de rebus honestis et / pertinentibus ad bene beateque vivendum, aut in studiis scientiae cognitionisque, / versatur. Cicero. (Printer's rule) Vol. I. [Vol. II] From October 1810, to March 1811, inclusive./ (Double rule) London: / Printed and Published by John Hunt, Examiner-Office, Beau- / fort Buildings, Strand: – Sold by J. Carpenter, Old Bond- / Street, and all Booksellers./ (Printer's rule) 1811.

The title page of Volume II of this printing is identical except for the one line which is changed to read "From March to December 1811 inclusive". The title page of the copy in the British Museum, printed sometime after August 23, 1812, modifies the description, omits the lines from Cicero, and adds the names of two more book-sellers, J. Miller, Bow Street, and Gale Curtis, Paternoster Row. The *Reflector* is now "A / Collection of Essays, / on Miscellaneous subjects of / Literature and Politics; / originally published as the commencement of a Quarterly Magazine, / and written by the Editor of the Examiner, / with the assistance of various other hands". This second binding also has a paragraph giving reasons for the publication's discontinuance. Pagination for the *Reflector* is as follows:

Vol. I – Title, verso blank. [i-ii]; Prospectus [iii] – ix, verso, Contents of No. 1; Text of numbers I and II, [1] – 486; the Contents of No. II, plus messages "To Correspondents", are printed on an unpaged leaf and inserted following page 248. Vol. II – Title, verso blank, [i-ii]; Contents of No. III, with a notice of apology for shortness of matter, [iii-iv]; Text of numbers III and IV, [1] – 503; the Contents of No. IV are printed on the recto of an unpaged leaf and inserted following page 216. There are errors in pagination in the fourth number: Pages

256-266 are omitted, pages 339-354 are repeated, and pages 500-503 rightly numbered would read 450-453. Page 446 is numbered 644. The first issue consists of 248 pages of material, the second 238, the third 216, and the fourth 243, a total of 945 pages, not counting the Prospectus, which is 6 pages.

The *Reflector* contains eighty-seven full-length articles and twenty-five short miscellaneous items, a total of one hundred twelve, of which ninety-four have been identified and eighteen remain anonymous. Of the unidentified articles, eleven are full-sized items and seven are among the miscellaneous items. The bound *Reflector* in the British Museum was helpful in the work of identification, for in it Hunt had pencilled the names of the writers of many of the articles, but some of the articles could be identified without his help.

When Hunt had assembled the material for the first issue of the *Reflector* in December 1810, he had contributions from at least eight people, seven of whom have been identified. Hunt leads with a total of nine articles, 108 pages, forty-three per cent of the issue – twice as much material as he was to write for any one subsequent issue. Two-thirds of his material is politically oriented, and to emphasize the importance of politics, the opening article takes a long-range view of politics in England in the preceding decade or so. The theatre is limited to his one Retrospect article, but the long essay on the state of the arts in England matches his opening political article. His translation of Voltaire's *Voyage de la Raison* and his continuation of the travels are politically motivated, but the "Account of a Familiar Spirit" is imaginative and didactic. Barnes, Dyer, and Field each have three articles, Aikin and Scholefield two each, and Gilchrist one; two items have not been identified. Only one article is signed with the writer's name, Octavius Gilchrist; the rest are anonymous or pseudonymous. For his signature Barron Field used three daggers; Barnes and Aikin used their initials, Dyer "An Observer", and Scholefield "Philo-Tragicus", "Vindex", and "S". One of the unidentified articles is not signed, while the other is signed "A Member of the Established Church". Charles Lamb does not appear in the first issue at all, but he did contribute fourteen items to the next three issues.[17] Hunt's associates in the first *Reflector* contributed articles of a miscellaneous nature. Dr. Aikin wrote on war and on manners and customs of fifty years ago; Field likewise assembled information on customs of past times and began his series of letters from a law student. Dyer wrote on public institutions, which he had been investigating, and on the claims of the Catholics, and began his series on the Constitution. Barnes and Gilchrist wrote on literature, and the unknown "Member of the Established Church" denounced the Methodists. The *Reflector* thus had considerable variety of subject matter on politics, the theatre, fine arts and *belles lettres* and should have attracted a wide intellectual audience.

A few days after publishing the first *Reflector*, Hunt was off for a five-day visit with Scholefield at Cambridge, writing descriptions of the town and university to Marianne back in Beckenham and apparently unconcerned about his new literary venture, since he did not mention it. He no doubt needed a holiday. He had not been well and the *Reflector* had been an added burden to him. An item in the *Examiner* early in November said that the "editor had been prevented by illness from attending the theatre the past week and from writing the usual article at the opening of this paper".[18] Thornton Hunt said that "It was in obedience to medical advice that he paid a visit in the earliest days of January to schoolfellows at Cambridge and Oxford."[19] Hunt also seems to have been unconcerned about the third libel action pending against him and his brother for reprinting, on September 2, 1810, an article titled "One Thousand Lashes!!" from the *Stamford News*. Their trial took place on February 22, 1811, before Lord Ellenborough with Brougham conducting their defense and Sir Vicary Gibbs as prosecutor. Though Drakard of the *News* was to be convicted for the same offense a few weeks later, the Hunts were acquitted. The first step in what was to be an important

17 Walter Graham, in *English Literary Periodicals* (New York, 1930), p. 142, says that "Lamb wrote seven out of twenty-four essays in the first number, and at least eight others before the end of the year", but this is an error.

18 *Examiner* (November 4, 1810), p. 691.

19 *The Correspondence of Leigh Hunt*, ed. Thornton Hunt (London, 1862), I, 47.

friendship in Hunt's life occurred on March 2, 1811, when Shelley wrote to Hunt congratulating him on his acquittal, just about three weeks before Shelley was expelled from Oxford for writing "The Necessity of Atheism". Meanwhile, the king was declared incapacitated, the Prince of Wales was installed as Prince Regent, and Henry Crabb Robinson began his very helpful *Diary*. On Thursday, April 11, Hunt's brother Robert was married to Miss Priscilla John of Stoke Newington and the marriage was duly noted in the following Sunday's *Examiner*.

An event of significance to literature took place sometime during the seven months when the second issue of the *Reflector* was in preparation, for during this period Lamb's connection with the *Reflector* began – and very likely the Lamb-Hunt friendship, which was to endure for many years and was to influence the development of the familiar essay, began at the same time. When the second issue was published on or about July 27, 1811, Lamb had contributed twenty pages of it: three personal essays and a one-page anecdote, beginning a trend toward the inclusion of more imaginative writing in the periodical. Another new writer was Thomas Mitchell, as well as an anonymous writer who was probably Robert Hunt. Dr. Aikin sent one of his many articles, and Barnes, Dyer, Field, and Scholefield also wrote for it. The first issue had elicited some response from its readers in the form of articles, and four of them were published in the second issue. Hunt also put in a half-page message "To Correspondents" telling "R.F.E." that his article would be published in the next number (which it was), turning down items from Mr. S. and Mr. B., and rejecting verses by "O.J." with an admonition to be more original: "Good imitation is a very good sign of success, but originality only is the attainment of it." Hunt was still the leading contributor but less extensively with only four items and part of another, totalling forty-one pages, and his first item is Article IX. Besides his "Retrospect" articles he has a political essay, his response to Barron Field's contribution on pruriency in literature, and his poem, "Politics and Poetics". Hunt was already depending heavily upon the assistance of others, a dependence which was to continue.

Sometime after the issuance of the second *Reflector* and probably early in September 1811, Hunt made the acquaintance of Thomas Moore, beginning a friendship which was to have its ups and downs over the years. Hunt sent Moore a copy of the second issue and Moore wrote to thank him for the magazine and to compliment him on the poem in it. A postscript indicates that Moore wrote something for the *Reflector*:

> The fragment which Carpenter [the bookseller] told you I had for the *Reflector* was *wickedly* political. Some of the allusions have now lost their hold, but you shall see it, and perhaps something may, with your assistance, be yet made of it.[20]

The "fragment" is probably the miscellaneous item in the third issue entitled "The Patriot's Almanac" and signed "Politician", though it does not now seem "wickedly political".

Beginning with the third issue, which came from the press on October 25, 1811, the magazine displayed a minor change in format, that of heading every second or right-hand page with the title of the article on that page. It was also the shortest of the four issues, only 216 pages, but with an increase (to ten) in the Short Miscellaneous Pieces. In a "Notice" prefixed to the issue Hunt said that the shortage of pages would be "made up in the next Publication", and "With the commencement of 1812, the REFLECTOR (in justice to its title) will put on more staid and quarterly habits, and it is trusted, that with the promises of fresh and valuable Correspondence with which the Proprietors have been gratified, their Magazine, like other wild beginners, will become better in every respect, as it acquires regularity." But the "wild beginner" remained erratic, for the fourth issue was delayed until nearly the end of March. The third *Reflector* continued the trends already established. The number of articles increased to twenty-nine, but they were shorter for the most part and more of them were anonymous. The most important items are, of course, Lamb's: the essays on Hogarth, on hissing at theatres, and on

[20] Thomas Moore, *Prose and Verse, Humorous, Satirical, and Sentimental* (New York, 1878), p. 310. Hunt had quoted Moore in the Dialogue (I, 24-26) and Moore was one of the four poets who received laurels in "Feast of the Poets" (II, 321).

burial societies. Hunt's thirty-seven pages included an important political item, "On the Present and Future Character of the Prince Regent", as the first article. Lucy Aikin's poem concludes the third issue, which also included contributions by her father, Barnes, Dyer, Field, Mitchell, and Scholefield.

The fourth *Reflector* was intended to conclude 1811, but it did not appear until March 23, 1812. The number of individual items had increased to thirty-two, seven of which are unidentified; the remainder are by the usual contributors, Hunt, Lamb, Aikin, Barnes, Dyer, Field, Mitchell, and Scholefield. Hunt's forty-three pages included two compositions which have remained among his most highly appreciated works, "The Feast of the Poets" and "A Day by the Fire". Lamb's forty-five pages are another kind of feast: the essay on Shakespeare, the poem "A Farewell to Tobacco", his "Specimens" of Fuller, and four personal essays. The contributions of Hunt and Lamb are alone enough to make this an outstanding issue, but it also contained satires by Barnes and Mitchell, personal essays by Aikin and Field, and articles on politics, education, and biography. Hunt evidently was not giving wholehearted attention to his editorial duties, for he overlooked several errors in pagination and in one case sixteen page numbers are repeated.

The fourth issue gave no indication that it was to be the last, but the Hunts must have made the decision to abandon or at least suspend publication at about this time and passed it to the contributors, for the serials were left unfinished and no articles intended for the *Reflector* appear in other papers. Hunt gives "want of funds" as the reason in his *Autobiography* and "limited means" in the introductory paragraph inserted before the Prospectus in the second binding of the magazine. Actually, the quality of the magazine was rising with every issue and circulation was increasing. The Hunts paid their contributors well, but their audience, mainly "radical reformers", was not then "sufficiently rich or numerous to support such a publication".[21] The depression of 1810-1812 may have been one reason for its suspension. But

[21] *Autobiography*, p. 214.

another event of March 1812 was to have a lasting effect upon the lives of the Hunts. The celebrated article which sent the brothers to prison, "The Prince on St. Patrick's Day", was published in the *Examiner* the day before the last *Reflector* appeared, and though their trial did not take place until nearly eight months later, on December 9, the expectation of its expense may have caused the retrenchment. The libel actions drained their finances, and Hunt, who had moved in November from Beckenham to 37 Portland Street, Hampstead, had overextended himself in furnishing his new place. Though he received some money from the estate of his American grandfather, Stephen Shewell, in 1811[22] and his income from the *Examiner* in 1811 was £511,[23] an upholsterer was pressing him for payment of a large bill, which he paid by means of a loan from Dr. Knighton.[24] The *Reflector* was not yet paying its own way, and the uncertainties of 1812 probably made John Hunt, the practical man of business, decide to give up the venture.

Because the introductory paragraph inserted in the second binding of the magazine and written late in 1812 when the circumstances of the discontinuance were fresh in Hunt's mind has not been reprinted, it is quoted in full:

It is but justice to this Publication, though a Work of very various merit, good, bad, and indifferent, to state, that as far as the limited means of the Proprietors could give it publicity, it met with the most promising encouragement, and that it was discontinued, partly by reason of the Editor's uneditorial want of attention to regularity of publication, but *chiefly* on account of those limited means. The Proprietors still think that a work of the kind would succeed, and have not given up the hope of reviving it some future day, though perhaps in a smaller form and with more select materials; but proper Contributors must be well paid, both out of policy and justice; and they plainly confess that they were unable to bear the expense. – Such as it is however, the work may be found not unworthy of additional readers. One of the Gentlemen who favoured it with their assistance,

[22] Stephen F. Fogle, "Leigh Hunt's Lost Brother and the American Legacy", *K-SJ*, VIII (1959), 99.

[23] George D. Stout, *Political History of Leigh Hunt's Examiner* (= *Washington University Studies, New Series, Language and Literature*, No. 19) (St. Louis, 1949).

[24] Brewer, pp. 88-89.

is a writer well-known and esteemed in the walks of criticism and rational philosophy, as the reader will surmise perhaps by the signature of J. A. affixed to some of his articles; and it is the Editor's particular pride and pleasure, that the largest and most entertaining part of it is in the production of a set of Persons, educated in one School, and valuable to each other for their friendship and congenial tastes.

The hope that the *Reflector* might be revived was not to be realized, however. Hunt's "pride and pleasure" in the contributions of his Christ's Hospital friends – which would include Lamb – is understandable, but the special mention of Dr. Aikin rather than Lamb would indicate that, in 1812, Hunt was as unaware of the genius of Lamb as he was of Wordsworth and Coleridge.

Thus ended the short life of the *Reflector*. Its discontinuance deprived both Lamb and Hunt of an outlet for their essays, though the *Examiner*, which became more of a literary repository after 1814, filled the void to some extent. The others in the coterie, more easily spared, continued in their chosen careers and are remembered today chiefly for their association with the *Reflector*. Landré believes (I, 63) that while the *Reflector* shows many of Hunt's brilliant qualities, it also shows his lack of balanced judgment and his ineptitude to conduct an undertaking of this sort, a conclusion that overlooks John Hunt's business acumen and places the entire responsibility on Leigh.

THE PROSPECTUS

In his Prospectus to the *Reflector* Hunt wrote that his new magazine would reflect the character of the times and be a "chronicle for posterity". He had already had practice in writing a prospectus, and this was not to be his last experience in this form of literature. Though he says that "of all pieces of fiction, the most amiable and the least interesting are Prospectuses", – and he quotes some standard phrases from prospectuses he had read – his composition is both amiable and interesting in its jibes at current magazines and its typically Huntian confidence that his magazine would be an improvement over the old ones. His *Reflector* would not stoop to the trivia to be found in other magazines: recipes, stale jests, plagiarism, and "a song about Phillis", among other things.

In order to be a chronicle for posterity, the *Reflector* would publish reports on politics, the theatre, and fine arts. "An essay or two upon Domestic or Foreign Policy" and a quarterly review of events would view the times with a historical perspective. Hunt did not pretend that he was politically unbiased; he wrote that the *Reflector* would emulate the *Examiner* in supporting Reform. But he was independent; since he did not know "a single politician personally", he could be totally independent in his opinions. He promised "comparative and didactic criticism" of the drama in the quarterly review of the theatricals. Theatres, he said, can be instructive as well as amusing, but in their present state "they show us neither what we are nor what we ought to be". As to the fine arts, he hoped to counteract Winckelmann's statement that the English lacked taste. Compared to the theatre, the fine arts were still in their infancy, but he praised the English school of painting which Reynolds, West, and others had developed. The *Reflector* would also contain miscellaneous literature on "Men and Manners, Enquiries into past and present Literature, and all subjects relative to Wit, Morals, and a true Refinement", and all articles would be original works which would portray the "mind" of the time.

As it turned out, Hunt's four categories did not receive equal coverage in the pages of his magazine. On the basis of space, 24% of the total of 945 pages was devoted to political items, 2% to the theatre, 28% to poetry and fine arts, 35% to miscellaneous literature, and 11% to personal essays. Hunt himself contributed 230 pages or 24% of the total, of which nearly half, 106 pages, were political essays, 18 were theatrical retrospects, 59 were fine arts and poetry, and 47 were personal essays. All but one is signed with his familiar indicator symbol.

THE POLITICAL ESSAYS

Volume I, No. 1: "The English Considered as a Thinking People, in Reference to Late Years"

"The Reformers; or, Wrongs of Intellect, – a Fragment of a Political Dialogue" (Unsigned)
"The Travels of Reason. Translated from the French of Voltaire, with a Continuation to the Present time"

Volume I, No. 2: "On the Public Spirit of the Times, and the State of the Parties"

Volume II, No. 3: "On the Present and Future Character of the Prince Regent"
"Retrospect of Public Affairs" (four essays)

Hunt promised his readers that each issue of the *Reflector* would have "an Essay or two" on politics, and he was true to his word, although their number decreased after the first issue.

The leading article in the first issue, "The English Considered as a Thinking People" (I, 1-16), is a sixteen-page (one sheet) essay in which he takes a long and critical look at England in 1810, pointing out flaws in its current political philosophy. England once had a reputation as a thinking nation (as contrasted with the fickle and vainglorious French), he writes, but their thinking power has been corrupted by flattery and by the substitution of the art of money-getting for other kinds of knowledge – that is, money has become a substitute for thinking. Hunt traces the political evils of the time to Pitt's fiscal and political policies and the system of faulty reasoning by which they have been defended and perpetuated. If a campaign fails, the politicians say that "statesmen, being mortals, cannot foresee"; their best hope for the future is that "something might turn up", a phrase that Hunt remembered and quoted when writing his *Autobiography* forty years later. Hunt uses facts, reason, and ridicule in criticizing the government's ineptitude, and the increase in the national debt and continued reverses in the war reinforce his assertions. He was understandably unhappy about Pitt's contempt for the liberal arts. Pitt could waste untold sums in unsuccessful military ventures and then say that "fine arts cannot be afforded". But if one criticizes the government, he is considered pro-Bonaparte and a traitor, more evidence of the corrupted thinking of the government. Hunt's panacea is "to turn again . . . to those intellectual studies and those reforms in our establishments, which shall prepare us for our own triumphs in return – the triumphs of philosophy and a wise freedom . . . in a word, to become once more a 'thinking' people". "The Reformists ask . . . only the renovation, in letter and in spirit, of that noble constitution." It is vain to say "that Reform will do no good; – the contrary has done a great deal of harm; and they have reason to try, as well as a right to demand, what their glorious ancestors bequeathed them" (I, 16).

The second article in the first issue, "The Reformers" (I, 17-28), does not bear a signature, nor is its authorship indicated in the British Museum copy of the *Reflector*, but Hunt is without doubt the author of this political dialogue. The place of importance assigned to the dialogue, following Hunt's opening essay, is a good indication that it was written by the editor. The dialogue was a popular essay form which Hunt used occasionally in his "Political Reflector" in the *Examiner*.[25] The anti-American sentiments in the essay coincide with Hunt's opinions. The essay bears the dateline "Utopia Lodge, March 1810" and is an outgrowth of an *Edinburgh Review* article which Hunt had answered in a series of essays in the *Examiner* the same month and published soon after in pamphlet form.[26]

The three speakers in the dialogue reveal that the Reformists do not agree as to the proper basis of representation in Parliament. None of them believe in giving the vote to the entire adult population, and the American system of giving the vote to the adult male population had resulted, according to such travelers as Isaac Weld and Thomas Moore, in "a general rottenness" and "political depravity". One speaker agrees with Sir Francis Burdett that property is the proper basis of political right and that the

[25] For example, "Dialogue Between a Corruptionist and a Reformist", *Examiner*, August 26, 1810.

[26] *Examiner*, March 18, 25, and April 1, 1810. The pamphlet was titled *The Reformist's Answer to the Article Entitled "State of Parties" in the last "Edinburgh Review" (No. 30), "By the Editor of the Examiner"*.

taxed male population should have the franchise. Another quotes the view of the *Edinburgh Review* that the rights of all people would be safeguarded if all classes were represented and if full freedom of speech prevailed, an extremely liberal view which was not to be realized for many years. This suggestion leads one speaker to suggest facetiously that all the arts and sciences should be represented in the House of Commons, mentioning Coleridge as the representative for literature.

The dialogue in the *Reflector* is a companion piece to Hunt's pamphlet and deserves a part of the credit given the pamphlet for its place in the reform movement. As Michael Roberts has pointed out,[27] the pamphlet gave Hunt's three suggestions for a reform program: he asked for a reduction in governmental expenditures, a more responsible ministry, and reform of Parliament, in addition to suggesting the union of the left-wing Whigs with the more moderate reformers and naming the leaders of both groups just as they are named in the *Reflector* article. By 1811 Hunt's demands coalesced into the single one of Parliamentary reform, but a merger along the lines suggested by Hunt took place in 1812 in the formation of the Hampden Club, a gathering of reformist forces.

By the time Hunt wrote his political essay for the second issue (I, 451-466), the Prince of Wales had become Prince Regent and had disappointed much of the country by retaining the former ministry and re-appointing his brother, the Duke of York, as commander of the army. The second essay continues the general comments of the first, observing deterioration in the areas of music, the drama, and politics, then building his discussion around the three political divisions of the country in 1811. The school of the Pittites has been able to maintain its stand from "the very uncommon want of discernment" and "a wayward imbecility of judgment" in George III (I, 455), and this continues Hunt's denunciation of the party of Pitt begun in his first essay. The Foxites or Whigs were in power briefly in 1806 but did not make full use of their opportunities for reform. They had some

[27] Michael Roberts, "Leigh Hunt's Place in the Reform Movement, 1808-1810", *RES*, XI (January 1935), 58-65.

liberal members who openly encouraged reform but now are weak and ineffectual. They need a leader, and Hunt suggests that the Prince should be that leader as well as a leader of all the people. The third political group, though not a party, is that of the Reformists, an important group with an ostensible leader in Sir Francis Burdett. But party lines have become somewhat obscured, and Hunt says that the two prominent groups could now be called Reformist and Corruptionist, with thinking persons on the side of reform.

Hunt's political writing in the year of the *Reflector* heaped more and more criticism on the Prince Regent, deplored his actions and his omissions, and reached a climax in the admittedly libelous *Examiner* article for which he was indicted. His third political essay (II, 1-13) is again in the prominent first position in the magazine and is devoted to "the present and future character of the Prince Regent". Hunt may have been somewhat foolhardy in attacking the Regent, but no one could say that he was not courageous. He begins the article with a fearless statement that he does not care for blame or praise, but "To write like Englishmen, and to endeavour that others may speak and act like Englishmen is our sole political object", to speak the truth regardless of consequences. He knows full well that the truth, in 1811, was no defense against libel. He is critical of those who praise the forty-seven-year-old prince and excuse his unprincely acts as part of his youthful spirits. Hunt says that the fall of many thrones in Europe should be a warning. He lists three actions by the Prince Regent which show "the nonexemption of princely intellects from weakness": his retaining of the old ministers, the reappointment of the Duke of York, and the two main social events so far in the Regent's reign – the Wimbledon Review and the Carlton House Fete. The Wimbledon Review had been delayed awaiting the Prince's convenience while the troops were badly needed in Portugal; the Fete was a taste-offending display. Both events were described in detail in the *Examiner* and in the "Retrospect" of the second issue of the *Reflector*. If such trends continue, Hunt warns, "the sound qualities of the English character are finally about to loosen and to rot, and that English independence will ere long be ripe for the gathering" (II, 13).

The three political essays and the four Retrospects are restatements of what Hunt had been saying in the *Examiner*. Hunt is consistent in his views. The essays are unified and progressive in their movement from the general situation to the parties to the Prince Regent as the principal target of his criticism. In his "Retrospect of Public Affairs" articles Hunt provides more of the true "chronicle" of the times, but not in the manner of some of the other magazines, which listed events in chronological order without comment. That chronology is valuable as a matter of record, but history is more than a series of dates. Hunt interprets events from the perspective of elapsed time. His Retrospects are skilfully written narratives interspersed with editorial comment, for reform is never far from the surface of things in Hunt's writings of this period.

To a limited extent the Retrospects can be used as evidence of the approximate terminal dates upon which they could have been written. The first Retrospect must have been written during the early part of December 1810. The latest event in the article can be pinpointed at November 29, the date on which parliament adjourned; the earliest event in the second Retrospect is the capture of the Isle of France on the same date, the news of which would not have been received for two or three weeks. Hunt states that "Such is the general state of affairs, abroad and at home, in this concluding month of the year 1810" (I, 242). Hunt saw little reason for optimism in the events of the last quarter of 1810. Napoleon was virtually unopposed anywhere on the continent; the Spanish were having trouble with their American colonies, and Hunt observed that only a more liberal policy would enable Spain to retain them. Napoleon's "continental system" was the cause of an increase in bankruptcies in England. The number of prosecutions for libel had increased, making the "boasted Freedom of the English Press" a trap to writers, and anyone who was personally obnoxious to the prosecutor could be the victim of a libel charge. The most important domestic event was the recurrence of the king's "mental malady", but it was not yet considered serious enough for Parliament to take up the regency. The fiftieth anniversary of the reign of George III, observed on November 1, and the death of Princess Amelia on November 2 are not mentioned. Hunt concludes with characteristic optimism as he points to the "healthful stamina in the British character and Constitution" and to the hope for Reform (I, 242).

The "Retrospects for Public Affairs" in the second and third issues (I, 440-451; II, 180-187) relate the events of the first and second calendar quarters of 1811. The Regency was established on December 31, 1810, and Hunt wrote that "it may now . . . be affirmed, that the reign of George III is concluded" (II, 182). On February 3 the Prince Regent was installed, and a little later he disappointed the country by retaining the ministry and reappointing the Duke of York as commander of the army despite the scandal under which he had recently resigned that post. The Carlton House Ball brought Hunt's advice "that the public esteem (if that is an object of his regard) is not to be obtained by gaudy shews" (II, 182). Informations *ex officio* against alleged libels had increased, but the law on flogging of military offenders had been modified. "The gloom created by the state of domestic affairs has been in some measure lightened by successes abroad" in the East Indies and in Portugal (I, 445). A son was born to Napoleon on March 20; the Duke of Gloucester was elected Chancellor of Cambridge on March 26. One of the several irritations which were to lead to war with America was reported: the *Little Belt* incident, an encounter between a British and an American ship.

Hunt prefaced the third *Reflector* with a notice informing readers "that the next Number will take up the three months that have been suffered to elapse during the publication, so as to make a half-yearly instead of a quarterly Retrospect, and enable the year to conclude with the second Volume, or four even Numbers, instead of dragging an odd one after it in consequence of the appearance of the first Number last winter". Consequently the fourth Retrospect covered the events of the last six months of 1811. The differences with America continued, Venezuela had declared its independence from Spain, and Wellington had some success in the Spanish peninsula. Business continued to suffer from the loss of European markets and frame-breaking had broken out in Nottingham. For the first time Hunt included sensational news, devoting a paragraph to two brutal murders which had caused great excitement in London in December 1811.

Hunt's translation of Voltaire's *Voyage de la Raison* and his political satire in the form of a continuation of the travels (I, 132-142) reflect his life-long veneration of Voltaire. Voltaire was a frequent subject of conversation with Hunt and his contemporaries, and Hunt tells us that he had an abridgment of the *Philosophical Dictionary* which he used as a kind of text book of opinion and style. Quotations from the *Dictionary* appear frequently in the *Examiner* and in the footnotes to this translation of the *Voyage*. In his *Autobiography* Hunt devotes five pages to Voltaire, whom he describes as France's greatest writer and the most prominent name in the entire eighteenth century.

Voltaire's little allegory concerns Reason and her daughter, Truth, who leave France because of "a curiosity in the present state of the political world" (I, 132). Wherever they go they are inclined to be impressed by fine courts – as was Voltaire – but they conclude that Toleration does exist in the world. Hunt's addition begins with the Reign of Terror, which causes Reason and Truth to flee to England where, "if little or nothing has been gained for civil liberty, a great deal has been gained for religious", and they decide that "if any country is ours, it is certainly that of Alfred, of Newton, and of Locke" (I, 146). Truth is last seen contentedly writing a history of recent years while Reason helps to inoculate children "with the discovery of Dr. Jenner" (I, 147). The observations of Reason and Truth in England are Hunt's own, and again he criticizes Pitt, who could make "continual ill-fortune pass for success" (I, 145).

While Hunt's political sentiments in the *Reflector* are the same as those in the *Examiner*, his writing is dignified, reasoned and reasonable, intellectual in orientation, appropriate to the "thinking man". The *Reflector* articles are not polemical or incendiary. The Hunt personality is still there in the sentiments, the easy prose, the confident statements, with a reserve and dignity appropriate to a magazine which is endeavoring to show the "mind" of its time.

THE THEATRICAL RETROSPECTS

Hunt's four "Retrospect of the Theatre" articles are essays rather than chronicles, occasionally approaching the personal essay for a paragraph or two. They are a general assessment of the theatre rather than reviews of particular plays or performances. Hunt is concerned with the theatres, the managers, the authors, and the state of the drama at the end of 1810: "Never has the history of the drama presented so fine an opening for rising talent" (I, 236). He attributes the deplorable state of the theatre to the increasing interest in politics, to the advance of commerce, and to a lowering of public taste by the many nouveau riche.

> It is universally agreed, that the Drama, with respect to intellect, is at the lowest point of degradation . . . Modern playwrights, in their inability to reach the arduous walks of writing, have agreed to sink into the lowest and easiest; . . . character has been degraded into caricature, plot and sentiment into common-place, wit into punning, and composition into sheer ignorance of the language. Comedy has become such mere farce, and the serious drama such mere floweriness, that criticism has for a long time had nothing to do but to quote repetitions, and to vary, if possible, its modes of contempt (I, 232).

Hunt particularly disapproved of the size of the royal theatres whose hugeness, he said, assisted in the deterioration of the drama, in building up a false taste, and in "the substitution of show for delicate acting"; the new Drury Lane Theatre, whose shows included performing horses, is "a bye-word in Europe for its horses and its asses" (I, 473). The "asses" (managers) offer farces which appeal to the lowest of their audiences; they care more for lucre than for art. Managers from Davenant to Sheridan "have done least for the advancement of the Drama", and the position of manager is most likely to fall to the person least fitted to conduct it (I, 234). The Haymarket Theatre (of which Colman was the manager at the time), "with its reasonable size, might become the very best in town", but for its "wretched and ruinous management" (II, 194). The crowds, the noise, the interruptions of the idlers, and the mediocrity of the stage fare make one unwilling to attend the theatre – and the picture he describes is worthy of Lamb:

> . . . a hundred authors, damned to no purpose, rise in grinning array before one; and the memory becomes one suffocating chaos of heat, weariness, noise of doors and benches, cries of the tap-room and the wheelbarrow, quarrelings, menaces, outcries, whistlings, shouts, groans, calls for apology, clattering of sticks, scraping of fiddles, prologues *in forma pauperis*, horrible dialogue on the stage and worse criticism in the boxes, puns, repetitions, roses and lilies, Irishmen, old England, – the man who, – and the trial by jury (I, 467).

The authors are all writing farces of questionable taste, each one imitating his predecessors with a "monotonous round of characters" and filling their plays with commonplace situations, puns, and claptrap, "as hacknied, as badly drawn, as fantastic and as unmeaning as the pictures upon a China dish" (II, 428). The offerings of Dibdin, Reynolds, Morton, and Clarke have little or nothing in them worthy of praise, but Thomas Moore's *M.P., or the Blue Stocking* is another matter. In the fourth *Reflector* Hunt says that the imitative portions of Moore's "opera" are "infinitely beneath" the author, but the small part which is original is by far the best:

> An immediate and striking superiority to the Dibdins and Reynoldses is observable in the commonest and most perverted efforts of a man of genius, even when he condescends to their level . . . The union of the lighter ethics with fanciful rhetoric and an air of accomplishment is still a desideratum in English poetry; the task seems peculiarly fitted to Mr. Moore. . . . It is not to be concluded, that the genius of Mr. Moore . . . would ever appear to advantage in the dramatic walk; – it is much more allied to description and fancy than passion and character (II, 431).

Hunt had expressed the same views in his long criticism in the *Examiner*[28] when *M.P.* was performed the previous September 9, and that critique is credited by Blunden and Landré[29] with being the occasion of the beginning of the Moore-Hunt acquaintance,

[28] *Examiner* (September 11, 1811), pp. 593-596.

[29] Edmund Blunden, *Leigh Hunt and His Circle* (New York and London, 1930), p. 70. Landré, I, 61.

although their correspondence began shortly before that time. Moore agreed with Hunt's verdict; *M.P.* was his last effort for the stage.

Hunt is pleased to report in his first *Reflector* article on the theatre that honest criticism is having an effect upon the public. Previously criticism was corrupt, "a mere matter of courtesy: an exchange of cards . . . the gradual migration of the critics from pit to boxes" (I, 234). Hunt himself was largely responsible for the "new criticism" of his day. When he began writing theatrical reviews for the *News* in 1805, he established the policy of complete independence which was to be continued in his political writing. As he wrote in his *Autobiography*, "To know an actor personally appeared to me a vice not to be thought of; and I would as lief have taken poison as accepted a ticket from the theatres."[30]

Because the plays of the time had so little in them worthy of comment and because of the tendency of the Romantic writers to concentrate more on people and characters than on the dramas themselves, Hunt's theatrical writings gave a vivid picture of the voices, gestures, even idiosyncrasies in pronunciation of the actors of his day, preserving to some extent the ephemeral nature of sound and sight now possible with motion pictures. His criticism became influential: Macready said that Hunt "seemed to hold my destinies in his grasp".[31] His analyses of performances "gave an altogether new scope and character to dramatic criticism".[32] William Archer stated that Hunt was the first dramatic critic of importance, that he was the only one of his day who produced criticism (as opposed to a mere review) which was authoritative and influential, but James Agate nominated Flecknoe for this distinction. Landré mentions Francis Gentleman, who in 1770 proposed "to give a concise general idea of the plays" in the same formula as Hunt.[33] Hunt's influence and importance have been

[30] *Autobiography*, p. 155.
[31] Blunden, p. 251.
[32] Louis Landré, "Leigh Hunt: His Contribution to English Romanticism", *K-SJ*, VIII (1959), 138.
[33] Landré, II, 101 note.

more far-reaching than those of his predecessors and the resemblance of his method to theirs is probably coincidental, since the situation in the early 1800's was clearly ripe for Hunt's style of theatrical criticism. As Blunden puts it, the value of Hunt's theatrical writing, for present-day readers, lies in his "entertaining precision in describing the habits, voices and faces of celebrated actors".[34] While the theatrical retrospects in the *Reflector* are limited in scope, they at least give a fair sample of Hunt's methods, talents, and attitudes.

THE FINE ARTS

Volume I, Number 1: "Remarks on the Past and Present State of the Arts in England"
"On the Spirit Proper for a Young Artist"

Volume I, Number 2: "Editor's reply to "Is it Justifiable to Reprint the Pruriencies of our Old Poets?"

Hunt fulfilled the promise in the Prospectus to give attention to the fine arts in his new magazine, not only in his long article discussing the state of the arts in England but in the many articles and essays by the various contributors. While Hunt lacked technical training in the visual arts (he was a pupil of his brother Robert for a short time), his innate esthetic sense and appreciation for things artistic was nurtured by his reading, his writing of prose and poetry, and his musical talent. His circle included artists, musicians, and poets, and that intercourse certainly enhanced his appreciation and power of expression. His brother Robert, the painter and engraver, wrote the fine arts essays for the *Examiner*; his old friend Henry Robertson reviewed concerts and operas. He knew the artist Henry Fuseli, but of primary importance in his knowledge and appreciation of art were the many hours, from childhood on, spent in the home and studio of his uncle, Benjamin West, president of the Royal Academy to his death in 1820 and the most prominent historical painter of

[34] Blunden, p. 43.

his day. Hunt had an ardent wish to improve the taste of his countrymen and to refute Winckelman's statement that England would always lack taste because of the nature of her climate. His fine arts essays merit close examination because his evaluation of the arts reveals his scope and capabilities, his habitual didactic and reforming zeal, and a judgment that has largely been confirmed by time.

Hunt unaccountably omitted articles on music from the *Reflector*, but music was a basis for his criticism of the visual arts. He wrote that he would apply the "general standard of poetry, music, and other works of genius; that is to say, by its invention, its harmony, and its nature" (I, 207). He declared that "unprofessional criticism" was of value in that it "shews unequivocally the popular progress of art" (I, 209). Hunt's zealous nature and his confidence in his own esthetic sense provided the urge to share his appreciation of literature, music, and art, and this side of his nature was even stronger than his reformist side. His "Remarks on the Past and Present State of the Arts in England" (I, 207-232) is a critique on fifty or more artists, architects, sculptors, and engravers, yet he did not raise a storm of protest from them – if he did, there is no record of it. Though Sir Joshua Reynolds, the founder of the British school of painting and of the Royal Academy, lacked originality, he was "a man of thinking and unshackled mind" with taste and "true greatness arising from simplicity" (I, 214). Benjamin West, he wrote, is 'the first historical artist who possessed a thorough knowledge of the human figure"; his paintings are "'calculated to make an admirer of poetry at once in love with painting"; he puts "fire and energy" in a noble countenance. But he "has great faults, particularly of manner", and his portrait painting is "utterly feeble and unsatisfactory" (I, 219). One wonders what West may have thought of his nephew's criticism. Fuseli, he said, is next to West in great works and before him in daring and imagination, but his coloring is bad, he sometimes gives himself up to "a cheap and perishing eccentricity", and some of his pictures are "outrages upon the human form" (I, 221). Thomas Stothard, to whom both Lamb and Hunt addressed poems, is praised for his "excellent simplicity" and censured for an unfinished look in his pictures (I, 222). Westall illustrated Mr. Walter Scott's *Marmion* – "and it is well that two clever men, so given up to a similar affectation, should go hand in hand and help to illustrate each other's faults" (I, 225). The best of the landscape painters is Turner (about whom Robert Hunt wrote in the *Examiner* the following June) [35] who uses indistinctness to achieve a "shadowy sublimity" of mist and distance (I, 230).

The names of Barry and Hogarth appear frequently in the *Reflector* because they were in the news in 1810. The *Edinburgh Review* of August and November 1810 carried reviews of the recently-published *Works of James Barry*, reviews which raised a controversy because of some of their aspersions. An anonymous article (probably by Robert Hunt) in the second *Reflector* refuted those aspersions, and Lamb contradicted some of Barry's remarks about Hogarth in his essay in the third issue. Hunt gives an evaluation of Barry's works in his essay and, in a footnote, disagrees with the reviewer's statement that pictures do not have a moral effect on the viewer. Editions of Hogarth's works were also published during these years and there was continuing discussion of their artistic merit and their morality. To Hunt Hogarth was more of a "wit and moral satirist upon canvas than a painter. . . . His great and unrivalled excellence lay in conveying the odiousness of vice by familiar touches"; he agreed with the consensus that Hogarth was a moral painter, though frequently approaching caricature. Hogarth's historical paintings, however, were vulgar and disgusting, "known only to be despised" (I, 213). Hunt and Lamb agree in regard to Barry, but their points of view are different. Hunt's article may have been partly responsible for Lamb's essay on Hogarth – and for their meeting in the first place.

According to Hunt, the leading sculptor of the day was Flaxman, who is met so often in Robinson's *Diary*. As to architecture, Hunt concludes that "either the architects have for centuries past had no acquaintance with invention, or invention has been en-

[35] *Examiner* (1811), p. 379.

tirely shut out of architecture" (I, 231); the new Drury Lane Theatre, by Smirke, is just "tasteful copying".

> Somerset House is light and elegant, but it is said to be ill built, and in a word, what beauty has it that is new? Mr. Soane, a theoretical master of his art, wished to be original when he repaired the Bank; and how did he effect his purpose? Merely by giving his edifice the look of a different object – merely by giving us a title-page contradictory to the contents of the book; the Bank has the air of a mausoleum, as if its builder intended to be ironical on our departed gold (I, 230).

Except for architecture, however, the English school of design abounds in originality, Hunt writes, and "the same spirit of thinking which has given freedom and variety to the English character . . . has entered into our composition as artists" (I, 231). Hunt closes with praise for a young art student, Benjamin Haydon (whose portrait of Hunt, painted ten years later, now hangs in the National Portrait Gallery): he has a "fine eye for correctness and colour, with an ambitious vehemence of style that promises grandeur of character but not refinement" (I, 231).

Although Hunt himself was only twenty-six, he did not hesitate to advise young artists on their proper "spirit", for "men of the most exalted genius . . . have been men of the most exalted spirit" (I, 131). A young artist should study the great poets and observe nature, but the main end of his art should be the advancement of his country's reputation – another expression of Hunt's defense of nationalism in art, a subject already touched upon in his essay on the state of the fine arts. "On the Spirit Proper for a Young Artist" (I, 125-131) contains two caveats for the young artist: He should avoid "a courtly notion of patronage, and a worldly notion of personal success" (I, 126). A patron is desirable as a means of support, but the artist should maintain his esthetic independence and remember that his real patron is posterity. Likewise, he should not be greedy. According to Hunt no one objects to the wise acquisition of wealth, but love of money can be corrupting, and Hunt's talent for aphorism comes into play here: "The best legacy a father can leave to his offspring is the ability to conquer fortune, not the leisure to be corrupted by it" (I, 130). Thus Hunt is concerned with the morality of the artist and of art, defending both against the "small thinkers" who see national decay in the rising interest in art. Art can "produce in us enlarged and honourable feelings, and . . . make us individually and therefore nationally good", and he summarizes the moral nature of art: "Nothing that is calculated to inspire us with the love of right, can in its nature be wrong" (I, 125).

Hunt was sparing of his literary criticism in the *Reflector*, if "The Feast of the Poets" is excluded from this category. In the second issue he contributed part of an article, the editor's reply to Barron Field's "dialogue" about reprinting the pruriencies of our older poets (I, 370-374). In an 1808 essay in the *Examiner* Hunt had written against the "Indecencies of our Dramatists" and was quoted by Field in his article. Hunt begins his reply with a generalization that "All writing is either for amusement or instruction; and in the case of the fine letters, generally for both" (I, 370). Instruction received from poetry can encourage morals, advance taste, and give information about former times. Though his comments concern pruriency, he passes over the morality of poetry, concluding that most of the great poets would suffer little expurgation since that would excise so small a part of their writings; furthermore, much of it is obscured by language – as in Chaucer's fabliaux, for example. He says that information about former times is not a valid defense as the information can be found in other sources. Then turning to Alexander Chalmers, whose *Works of the English Poets* touched off the discussion, he concludes with a blow at Chalmers' critical comments: They are "maudlin and superficial" and he has no right to tell anyone who the English poets are (I, 374). One senses here the implication that Hunt has that right, the *ex cathedra* pronouncement which irritated friends and enemies alike, but writers of the time tended to be dogmatic and to have a conceited regard for their own opinions.

THE POETRY

Volume I, Number 1: "Atys the Enthusiast: A Dithyrambic Poem Translated from Catullus, with Prefatory Remarks"

Volume I, Number 2: "Politics and Poetics, Or the Desperate Situation of a Journalist Unhappily Smitten with the Love of Rhyme"

Volume II, Number 4: "The Feast of the Poets"

Hunt's translations illustrate the breadth of his literary accomplishments and his propensity for sharing the good things of literature with his readers. Amy Lowell called Hunt "a great introducer" with a "touchstone mind; he knew instinctively what was good and never feared to proclaim it".[36] C. D. Thorpe awards Hunt first place among the translators of the Romantic period and one of the first three or four places among all English translators.[37] The first number of the *Reflector* contained Hunt's only translations in the four issues, the *Travels of Reason* from Voltaire and "Atys the Enthusiast" from Catullus (I, 165-174).

The story of Atys is unpleasant, for Atys emasculated himself in order to subdue his passions and then formed a fanatical sect in honor of Cybele. Though the act of emasculation is recounted quite frankly: "with flinty knife he gave to earth the weights that stamp virility", Hunt insists that it is not a poem "of a loose tendency", for if it had been it would not have been published in the *Reflector*. He says that "there is no poem of the same brevity that unites with so powerful an effect the two great tragic requisites of pity and terror" (I, 165, 166). In order to avoid the "gross violation of decency" of the French versions of Catullus, Hunt made two changes, omitting an allusion to a custom which "neither our manners nor morals should endure to hear" and using the pronoun *it* rather than the feminine pronoun to indicate

36 Amy Lowell, *John Keats* (Boston and New York, 1925), p. 136.

37 Clarence DeWitt Thorpe, "Leigh Hunt as Man of Letters: An Essay in Evaluation", in *Leigh Hunt's Literary Criticism*, ed. Lawrence Huston Houtchens and Carolyn Washburn Houtchens (New York, 1956), p. 14.

Atys' change to "a man without sex" (I, 172). This is undoubtedly the portion of the translation that the writer in the *Satirist,* under the title "Elegancies of Literature", particularly criticized: "I presume no one will venture to say that the translation is for the eye of any female." [38]

In the short preface to the poem Hunt explained his treatment of the poem and commented on its versification. He did not believe in following the original poem too closely in his translation but varied the length of the lines according to the mood or spirit of each section of the poem. The first part is all hurry and movement, for which Hunt uses an eight-foot line, which he says is much better than the "hopping solemnity" of Alexandrines (I, 168). The calm second section of the poem, after Atys has slept, is in the "solemnity" of hexameter, and later, when madness comes to Atys, pentameter and tetrameter lines show his agitation. Thus a meaningful contrast between sections of the poem is appropriate to the spirit of each section. Hunt defended his use of irregularity of versification – the variations in line length, occasional triplets, and off-rhyme – as especially suitable for rendering the "reckless vigour of the original", and he uses Dryden, whom he was studying at the time, as justification. He concludes his preface with the suggestion that "our versification would perhaps be rather improved than injured by looking back to the style of Dryden" (I, 169). Though "Atys" has some of Hunt's usual faults of diction, especially the adjective ending in -y, his diction contributes to mood, sound, and movement.

Hunt's first original poetry in the *Reflector* is the autobiographical "Politics and Poetics" (I, 361-365). The task of meeting a deadline with his weekly *Examiner* articles was always a problem for the easy-going and often poorly-organized Hunt, and these circumstances were not conducive to writing poetry. In the poem Hunt is pulled in two directions. His work table is covered with pamphlets, journals, letters, and material for his articles, while "poor old Homer", Milton, and Tasso are neglected. Nightmare (which is to appear in a *Reflector* essay also) will seize him if he falls asleep; he is bothered with headaches.

[38] *The Satirist*, p. 125.

"The Devil who comes for copy" is very punctual. He would like to be taken away by his Muse to "a seat in some poetic nook", which is described in terms reminiscent of Coleridge's "This Lime-Tree Bower My Prison". But he has to return to the reality of "scandals and jails", and he says farewell to his Muse.

Landré calls the poem "une confession amusée, mais néanmoins sincère".[39] Certainly it is amazingly prophetic in three of its lines, the first of which reflects his fondness for Spenser:

> And lo, my Bow'r of Bliss is turn'd into a jail!
>
> Th' enduring soul, that, to keep others free,
> Dares to give up its darling liberty. . . . (I, 364)

Two years later Hunt and his brother were to give up their liberty and go to jail for two years, and Hunt converted his rooms at Surrey Gaol into something like a bower with his books and his flowered wallpaper. His continuing bouts with the government and with libel suits are also mentioned:

> Let me but name the court, they swear and curse,
> And din me with hard names; and what is worse,
> 'Tis now three times that I have miss'd my purse. (I, 362)

The last line refers to the three libel actions which had cost Hunt about £100 each. Literary and political critic that he is, Hunt cannot resist inserting jabs at Gifford, Sheridan, and Canning; and Walter Scott writes "Of spears, plaids, bugles, helms, and border-wits" with "the worn-out sword he wields for pen" (I, 363).

The Dryden influence is apparent in the heroic couplets with the occasional triplet marked with heavy brackets. Hunt achieves variety in the lines by using occasional spondees and Alexandrines, double and triple rhymes, internal rhyme, and some feminine endings. In structure the poem is *a b a*, beginning with the everyday world of the journalist, moving to the imaginary bower, and returning to duty and reality at the end. The poem pleased Thomas Moore, who mentions it in one of his earliest letters to Hunt in September 1811, before the two had met. Moore's comments would indicate that he admired the parts of the poem which most nearly resembled his own flowery verses.[40]

[39] Landré, II, 227.
[40] Moore, p. 392.

"The Feast of the Poets" (II, 313-323), which Hunt calls his *jeu d'esprit* in his *Autobiography*, is one of his most important – and notorious – poems, and its three versions have received critical attention which makes detailed analysis unnecessary here. In 1810 Hunt had planned to write his "Planet of the Poets", which showed the influence of Dante and Chaucer: the poet is transported by his Muse to Venus, where departed poets reside. He abandoned the "Planet" for the "Feast" and substituted contemporary poets for those who were already dead. The device of a gathering of poets, modeled on Suckling's 1637 poem, "A Session of the Poets", is a handy and flexible one for critical or satiric handling of a number of writers, as Hunt's successive versions of the poem testify. The third version (1815) reflected his changed and changing views of Wordsworth, Coleridge, Scott, and others; its preface and notes, exceedingly brief in the *Reflector,* were enlarged to a defensive 125 pages, five times as long as the poem itself. Thorpe says that the "Feast" was written under the influence of Byron and is "a significant link in a chain of revealing evidence . . . in which we may plainly observe the progress of the vigorous critical conflict through which Hunt passed in arriving at his more favorable view of Wordsworth".[41] The bouncing anapestic tetrameter was an ideal choice for the almost frivolous fable of the poem, its movement and levity appropriate for the brief and superficial sketches of the parade of poets. This facility and superficiality distinguish Hunt's satire from that of Pope. His satire wounds without cutting deeply, and his portraits are caricatures. Most important is the revelation that in 1811 Hunt could crown Campbell, Southey, Scott, and Moore as the leading poets in a day which had seen the publication of the best of Wordsworth, Coleridge, Blake, and Burns. The Hunt of 1811 was not the discerning critic he was to become four or five years later when he championed Shelley and Keats, but his preoccupation with reform could blind him to the literary merits of a Tory poet. At least Hunt had the courage and honesty to admit his errors. Subsequent versions of the "Feast" gave due recognition to Wordsworth, Coleridge, Scott, and Landor; and Hunt made

[41] Thorpe, p. 33.

ample restitution to all four in his critical writings of later years. One opinion which was not to be moderated by time and maturity was his aversion for Gifford, the "sour little gentleman" who was not qualified to attend the feast of poets, since he was one of the "small critics, however well known" (II, 316). Fifty years later Hunt could write that Gifford was "the only man I ever attacked, respecting whom I felt no regret".[42]

The brevity of each caricature in the "Feast" and the needs of satire to focus on a subject's faults account in large measure for Hunt's errors of judgment in the poem. What he said was true, but in most cases it was only part of the picture. Wordsworth's subject matter was often that which other poets would reject; Coleridge's lectures were often rambling and unsatisfactory, as we know from Crabb Robinson's reports; Scott did seem to have an "innate and trusting reverence for thrones" (II, 316 note); Campbell's versification did lack invention. Most damaging is Hunt's later admission that he wrote with incomplete knowledge gathered primarily from second hand: "... laughing at Wordsworth, with whose writings I was then unacquainted, except through the medium of his deriders"[43] – this some thirteen years afters the publication of the *Lyrical Ballads* and four years after *Poems in Two Volumes*. Since Lamb and Wordsworth were such good friends for so many years, Hunt's ignorance of Wordsworth is a strong indication that Lamb and Hunt were not acquainted prior to the *Reflector* years, and surprisingly his acquaintance with Lamb in 1811 had not yet produced a more enlarged appreciation of Wordsworth. On the positive side, however, the poem shows Hunt's continuing appreciation for Shakespeare, Chaucer, Spenser, Milton, and Dryden, though Pope's followers were incensed at the line about his "cuckoo-song verses, one up and one down" (II, 314).

The immediate reaction to the "Feast" was not very pronounced. Even the *Satirist* ignored it until it came out separately in 1814. Hunt wrote that "the *Edinburgh Review* took no notice of the *Feast of the Poets,* though my verses praised it at the ex-

[42] *Autobiography*, p. 217.
[43] *Ibid.*, p. 223.

pense of the *Quarterly*, and though some of the reviewers, to my knowledge, liked it, and it echoed the opinions of others".[44] Mitchell, to whom the separate volume was dedicated, wrote Hunt that while they might not agree about the versification in the poem, he liked "the care and sprightliness which the versification of the Feast exhibits; there is an enjouement about it such as fresh verdure and a warm sun engender on a sparkling imagination".[45]

Hunt was to learn, with maturity, that one cannot raise himself by pulling others down, and he did not become a great writer of satires by criticizing Pope nor a great critic as a result of his *jeu d'esprit*. He did attain notoriety; he offended many people unnecessarily, more from arrogance than from a well-balanced love of the truth; he made questionable judgments which he had to retract; and he did not enhance his stature as a poet, even though he indicated in the poem that he considered himself below those he satirized because he was not among those invited to the feast. Satire sometimes turns on its creator, causing him more discomfort than his victims. Hunt admitted in his *Autobiography* that the poem "made almost every living poet and poetaster my enemy".[46] The ill-will that it generated, coupled with Hunt's reformist agitation and attacks on the government, was responsible for many of the later attacks upon him. To Blunden the "Feast" shows Hunt's "ambition and effort moving away from the political and dramatic contest to the literary arena; it records his principles and tastes in development; and it was one of his many pugnacious feats for the furtherance of what he thought truth and light."[47] Thus while posterity is amused by "The Feast of the Poets" in its original version and can use hindsight to attain perspective in considering it, the poem remains essentially negative, destructive, and superficial.[48]

[44] *Ibid.*, p. 227.
[45] Landré, II, 249 note.
[46] *Autobiography*, p. 215.
[47] Blunden, p. 65.
[48] For Hunt's treatment of Wordsworth and Coleridge in detail, see George D. Stout, "Leigh Hunt on Wordsworth and Coleridge", *K-SJ*, VI (1957), 59-73.

THE PERSONAL ESSAYS

Volume I, Number 1: "Account of a Familiar Spirit, Who Visited and Conversed with the Author in a Manner Equally New and Forcible, Shewing the Carnivorous Duties of All Rational Beings and the True End of Philosophy"

Volume II, Number 3: "ψυχης Ιατρειον: or an Analogical Essay on the Treatment of Intellectual Disorders, Together with an Account of a Surprising Cure Performed Therein by the Writer When Asleep"
"The True Enjoyment of Splendour: – A Chinese Apologue"

Volume II, Number 4: "A Day by the Fire, – Poetically and Practically Considered"

Hunt's four personal essays in the *Reflector* follow in the tradition of Addison and the eighteenth century periodical essayists, but in their abandonment of anonymity they are transitional. They are signed with Hunt's familiar indicator, and he speaks of himself as the *Reflector,* but never does Mr. Reflector become a persona, a separate individualized character or mouthpiece distinct from Hunt – it is always Hunt expressing his own individual personality and attitudes, likes and dislikes. The dream or vision, borrowed from Addison but going back to Chaucer and before, is used in two of the essays; in one he used the oriental tale, another device borrowed from his predecessors. But unlike his predecessors, Hunt moralizes very little in his personal essays; rather he communicates a sense of pleasure and enjoyment arising from his broad catholicity of taste. For the most part the essays are chatty and colloquial, entertaining and interesting; they are heavily detailed and show Hunt's facile, extended style that contrasts so sharply with Lamb's more concise writing. They are rich in allusions and quotations, some of them facetious; topical references tend to destroy the timelessness and universality expected in a good essay. They also show Hunt's failure to refine his ore assiduously, and often they are reminders of Hunt, the political essayist.

The "Account of a Familiar Spirit" (I, 86-99) is a traditional essay employing the dream device as a means of introducing a persona to express the author's opinions. When the essay was reprinted in Hazlitt's collection of essays, *The Round Table*, in 1817, it was retitled more succinctly "On the Night-Mare". It combines the informative and didactic essay with the imagination and erudition of a poetic nature. After a long preface, another structural habit of the times, he discusses supernatural spirits (such as Bickerstaff's Pacolet) and foods as inducers of dreams and visions, then recounts his dream. The Prince of the Nightmares materializes out of the remains of a supper; with this gregarious spirit Hunt has a long conversation filled with allusions ranging from Solomon to Napoleon. The Nightmare tells him that disturbed digestions and guilty consciences account for the troubles of great men of history. Even the *Edinburgh Reviewers* are "unable to digest the least thing that disagrees with them"; the spirit nearly suffocated a Reviewer recently "in the shape of a Reformist" (I, 98). He tells Hunt to inform his countrymen that their habits of feasting on all occasions is neither philosophic nor politic; they should give more attention to the good of their country. The description of the spirit is particularly vivid, especially its parting laugh, "a compound of the gabblings of geese, grunting of hogs, quacking of ducks, squabbling of turkies, and a winding up of smoke-jacks" (I, 99). Hunt resembles Lamb in this piling up of similes to intensify a description, expanding it but not contributing to the advance or progress of the essay.

By facetiously attributing many of the world's ills to intemperate diet, Hunt underscores and illuminates some of those ills. This is Hunt the social satirist speaking, but it is also Hunt the hypochondriac. His health, never very good, was not helped by his experiments with special diets of his own concoction. Thornton Hunt spoke of the "excessive spareness of diet which he adopted, partly from a blind belief in the virtues of temperance under every aspect".[49] The "Account of a Familiar Spirit" is topical, didactic, and personal, but the personal element is subordinate to its social criticism.

"PSUKES IATREION" (A Place of Healing for the Soul), subtitled an "Analogical Essay on the Treatment of Intellectual Disorders, together with an Account of a surprising Cure performed therein by the Writer when asleep" (I, 144-156), continues to reflect Hunt's preoccupation with health, in this case the individual's mental health, suggesting a doctor for mental disturbances, a kind of psychological consultant or diagnostician. Again the essay is imitative in its long introduction, the allusions, quotations, and topical references; he discusses the ill-tempered, the envious, and the miserly in what are almost short "characters", then gives his prescriptions for their cures. Another dream follows, "one of my usual reveries", as he calls it, in which he is a "mental doctor" who cures an ill-tempered man by finding the basic cause of his bad temper: a pin. Again he attributes the troubles of the world to minor irritations which can be overcome by temperance and common sense, and Hunt is the doctor who can prescribe for the world's ills. After curing his patient, he calls on another disagreeable man, the Attorney General, who is "writhing under a newspaper attack", probably by the *Examiner* (II, 156). The Attorney General is Sir Vicary Gibbs, also known as "Vinegar Gibbs", the man who brought the libel charges against the Hunts. This visit is not reported; the light touch is enough to imply clearly that Gibbs is in need of a mental doctor.

Hunt's little Chinese apologue, "The True Enjoyment of Splendour" (II, 195-197), one of the miscellaneous items in the third issue of the *Reflector*, is not one of his best efforts. Because of its topical nature, it was not reprinted by Hunt, but had to wait until 1891 for reprinting in Johnson's *Essays of Leigh Hunt*. The oriental tale was an old device of Goldsmith and other eighteenth century essayists, and Hunt's is in the usual pseudo-oriental language, stilted, unnatural, and sententious. Hunt's apologue is a thinly-disguised criticism of the Prince Regent, who is called Quo and is handsome, corpulent, and without dignity. This imaginative

49 *Correspondence*, I, 47.

tale is plainly political, with brevity as its best quality. When the Prince Regent reviewed the troops at Wimbledon on June 14, 1811, he wore a particularly magnificent uniform, made expressly for the occasion at great cost, and he was severely criticized for it in the *Reflector* (II, 11). In the tale Quo walks through the streets of Pekin in a magnificent costume covered with jewels from cap to shoes. The moral of the piece, that the prince should curtail his spending and love of show, is contained in the speech of the Bonze, who could be any of the reformists, including Hunt himself. He says that Quo "has taken infinite labour to acquire his magnificence, he takes still greater pains to preserve it, and all the while, I, who am lying under a shed, enjoy it for nothing" (II, 197).

Hunt's long personal essay, "A Day by the Fire" (II, 400-419), which was also reprinted in *The Round Table*, is a fitting crown to his *Reflector* writing. It is his finest prose composition of the period, and it has enjoyed well-deserved appreciation of his readers. Even more than Lamb's personal essays in the *Reflector*, it marks a midway point between the traditional and the full-fledged personal or familiar essay. We have the subjective self-revelation which is a trademark of the familiar essay of the twenties and none of the façade, the fictitious character, of the traditional essay. This is Hunt himself speaking, a "man speaking to men". The reader is taken into Hunt's living room, with its fire, the urn, the books, chairs, and windows; there is the cosy ("snug" is the word he uses) secure feeling of a warm, comfortable room sheltered from the chill of the world outside the windows and a friendly, warm-hearted man as the reader's companion. In the discursive style, the chatty, intimate conversational writing, Hunt and the reader spend a day together in the same close contact he often achieved, a kind of arm-in-arm stroll, a "saunter" through the day with a charming, cultivated, friendly man.

The spatial freedom of the *Reflector's* pages was conducive to writing an essay like "A Day by the Fire". The slow, almost imperceptible movement of the essay conveys the slow movement of time as the day creeps from morning to night, just as an inactive, reflective day spent indoors can be, with the passing of time marked only by the meals and the ticking of a clock. In this leisurely setting the fireplace and the urn become companionable, contributing to the comfort and the slight action in the room, and perception of small details is more keen: the reddening of the coals when prodded with the poker; the steaming, the bubbling, and even the aloof pride of the urn. The outer world penetrates but dimly as the Reflector relaxes with the reader beside him and lets his mind move from one thought to another in its strange associative processes. "The thought roves about into a hundred abstractions, some of them suggested by the fire, – some of them suggested by that suggestion, – some of them arising from the general sensation of comfort and composure" (II, 411). The urn brings to mind Cowper, "the poet of quiet life and familiar observation", and his "bubbling and loud-hissing urn" (II, 400), but this is only a beginning. As the discourse proceeds, it becomes rich with quotations and allusions brought to mind by thoughts in the comfort of the room: Chaucer, Spenser, Dryden, Milton, Drayton, Horace; the fabric of the essay takes on a depth or thickness, a growth or development beyond the chattiness of the beginning. Again we have Hunt the introducer, the man of charm and erudition who shares the good things of his life with his readers, motivated by his generous nature and by a desire to improve the taste of his countrymen.

The first sentence establishes the personal nature of the essay: "I am one of those that delight in a fireside, and can enjoy it without even the help of a cat or a tea-kettle" (II, 400). Hunt coined the word "Firesider" in this essay,[50] and it came to be associated with Hunt and the personal nature of his essays, his habit of taking his reader along with him, not only on his saunters, but into his study as well. In the quiet seclusion of his day by the fire, the senses are highly perceptive: sounds become events – the dustman's bell, the clash of milk pails, the hissing urn, the "roaring flame" that "mounts aloft with a deep and fitful sound as of a shaken carpet" (II, 402). Hunt observes that he "was

[50] The *O.E.D.* lists the word as a nonce-word from Hazlitt's *Round Table*, 1817, quoted by the reviewer in *Quarterly Review* (xvii, 157) as a coinage by Hazlitt – an error, of course.

always reckoned a lively hand at a simile", and this essay is replete with this handy device for conveying difficult impressions. For example, in bad weather he feels "a heavy sky go over me like a featherbed, or rather like a huge brush which rubs all my nap the wrong way" (II, 401).

The reactions, the impressions, the opinions are all Hunt's and some of the allusions tie the essay to Hunt's other writings. The reader acquiesces willingly as Hunt pauses over an especially apt word like *snug*, "that soul-wrapping epithet", or a resentful thought of Winckelmann's calumnies on England's climate, or a paragraph on the personality of the urn. While this essay is the most personal of the four in the *Reflector*, showing Hunt's sedentary life, his taste, his love of companionship, it lacks the egoism, the nostalgia, the pathos or whimsy of the later fully-developed familiar essays, and Hunt was never to become the familiar essayist that Lamb was. But in 1812 Hunt was a step ahead of Lamb, for "A Day by the Fire" is the best example of transition in the development of the familiar essay,[51] reflecting the subjective nature of the Romantics and helping to pave the way for what was to come in the 1820's.

In the *Reflector* Hunt is still the political essayist of the *Examiner* preoccupied with the affairs of the day, but he is also the poet, the translator, and writer of personal essays. In his Prospectus he wrote that politics was having an effect upon literature, for it contains "the seeds of the most flourishing and refreshing arts",[52] and Hunt's imaginative writing includes enough topical references to illustrate this statement. Some of Hunt's *Reflector* writing is a repetition of what he had said in his weekly paper, for its avowed purpose was to be a chronicle, but the personality is different, as if Hunt removed his *Examiner*'s smock for the *Reflector*'s smoking jacket. Mr. Reflector has a greater sobriety, a self-conscious dignity, an awareness that he is writing for a medium with more status and permanence. He is still the same scholarly person, just as opinionated as Mr. Examiner, and the opinions are the same,

51 Watson, p. 76.
52 Prospectus, p. v.

but he is less polemical and more subtle, less exclamatory and more reasonable. The writing is still that of a man who has read widely and remembered well and whose greatest pleasure, next, perhaps, to convincing his readers of the necessity for reform, is in sharing his erudition. Mr. Reflector is a more amiable companion than Mr. Examiner, and in this amiability lies much of the charm of Hunt's writing in the *Reflector*.

III

CHARLES LAMB AND HIS *REFLECTOR* ESSAYS

Charles Lamb was thirty-five years old and had been a clerk in the accounting office at East India House for eighteen years when the first issue of the *Reflector* was published around New Year's Day, 1811. His annual salary was £160 plus overtime,[1] but he was always plagued by the necessity of increasing his income: "I must do something for money", he wrote to Coleridge in 1809.[2] He had tried his hand at a number of things: poetry, plays, essays, newspaper work. He and Mary had collaborated on their *Tales from Shakespeare* (1807) for Godwin, and in 1808 Lamb's *Specimens of English Dramatic Poets Who Lived about the Time of Shakespeare*, which he had been collecting since 1796 in the British Museum, was published by Longmans. The year 1809 saw the publication of *Poetry for Children*, a joint effort of Charles, Mary and John Lamb. In June of that year Charles and Mary moved from Mitre Court Buildings, where they had lived since 1801, to Inner Temple Lane, which was to be their home until the fall of 1817. Their vacations of 1809 and 1810 were spent in Wiltshire with the Hazlitts, but the 1811 holiday was spent in town. Mary's mental and physical health was always precarious, though she lived to be eighty-two, and she was in poor health late in 1810 when both she and Charles were on their water diet. Lamb's "evenings", the Wednesday evenings – later moved to Thursday – when he was at home to his friends, seem

[1] E. V. Lucas, *The Life of Charles Lamb* (New York and London, 1907), I, 409.

[2] *The Letters of Charles Lamb, to which are added those of his sister Mary Lamb*, ed. E. V. Lucas (London, 1935), II, 74.

Charles Lamb in 1804

(Painting by William Hazlitt)
(Copyright, National Portrait Gallery)

to have been dropped in 1810 for fortnightly gatherings, probably because of Mary's health, but they were resumed the following July. These were busy years for the Lambs, and they must have written many letters, but few have survived: something like six for 1811, three for 1812, and none for 1813. None of them mentions the *Reflector* or Lamb's essays in it. Without Crabb Robinson's diary we would know little of their activities for 1811. Although Charles' days were busy ones at the East India House, that year he published *Prince Dorus* and furnished Hunt with his fourteen *Reflector* essays.

Life had not been particularly kind to Lamb in the years since he left Christ's Hospital, but his ebullient nature had a spark of humor and vivacity which the buffetings of life could not quench. The tragic year of 1796, when Mary killed their mother in a moment of insanity, and the years of care and uncertainty with Mary, were bound to leave their sobering and maturing mark on the young man. Finances were always a severe problem; and while the clerical drudgery at East India House must have been somewhat of a depressant, it also contributed to the storehouse of experience upon which he was to draw in some of his writing. The hours and years spent in antiquarian research left a mark on his critical perception as well as on his prose style. Life was kindest to Lamb in giving him a capacity for friendship and a genius for attracting and holding friends, qualities revealed in the interchange of conversation and correspondence with Coleridge, Wordsworth, Godwin, Dyer, Robinson, Hazlitt, and many others. The ferment of ideas within and surrounding Lamb and his friends helped to produce the many facets of the Romantic Period, to give it the depth and breadth it acquired from Europe, to enhance its liberalizing tendencies, and much more. The personality and the fine intellect of Charles Lamb may have been a principal catalyst in the curious compound that is Romanticism.

A question which seems fated to go unanswered until new information comes to light concerns the first meeting of Leigh Hunt and Charles Lamb. On the basis of available information it would appear that they were brought together by the *Reflector* in the early months of 1811. Blunden says that the two men were friends by 1810 but does not give evidence.[3] Neither Landré nor Lucas speculates about the date, but Landré thinks that they may have met through Barron Field, Lucas that they met through John Lamb.[4] Hunt is of no help. Lamb, who was ten years his senior, had left Christ's Hospital two years before Hunt arrived there, but Hunt recalled seeing Lamb on those occasions when Lamb returned to the school for visits with old friends. Since he does not say that they met or conversed, the assumption is that they did not, for ten years' difference in ages is usually insurmountable at that time of life. Lamb next appears in the *Autobiography* as a contributor to the *Reflector*. Since both men were publishing by 1811 and Hunt was well known as the editor of the *Examiner*, each would have been aware of the other's existence, even if they were not acquainted. Actually, with their common background in Christ's Hospital, their mutual interest in literature and the drama, and the possibility of several mutual acquaintances, it seems incredible that they were not friends for ten years before the *Reflector* first appeared. But neither man mentions the other in any extant correspondence of the period nor are they connected in any way in the correspondence of their friends. Unreasonable as it seems, the fact remains that no evidence exists of any social intercourse between Lamb and Hunt until the *Reflector* was expiring.

Although both men were prominent enough to have become acquainted without an intermediary, a mutual acquaintance could have brought them together. Lucas' suggestion that they met through John Lamb is based on John's subscription to Hunt's *Juvenilia* (1801), but being a subscriber is not evidence of friendship, since Hunt's father obtained the subscriptions. Also, John Lamb is an unlikely candidate since no evidence exists of friendship between him and Hunt. Another *Juvenilia* subscriber would be as likely a connection: Barron Field. Field was only fifteen at the time, and how he happened to subscribe to this first book by an unknown prodigy is another mystery. Perhaps Hunt's father knew Field's father, who may have subscribed in his son's name.

[3] Blunden, p. 56.

[4] Landré, I, 60; *Life*, I, 417.

At any rate, Barron Field's name is in the first and second, but not in the subsequent, editions.[5] Field would have been of the right age to have been a Bluecoat Boy before Hunt left Christ's Hospital, but he was never enrolled as a student there. The possibility exists that he may have been a special student like his younger brother Frederick, but the fact that there is no mention of it anywhere seems to eliminate this possibility. Field and Hunt were well acquainted by the beginning of 1804, when Field was seventeen and Hunt nineteen, for Hunt mentions him in a letter to Marianne dated February 23, 1804. Field's brother Francis was a co-worker of Lamb's at the East India House office, and he may have taken Lamb home with him. If so, he may have met Hunt there at any time from early 1804 on. Or, Lamb and Field may have met in 1809 after the Lambs moved to Number 4 Inner Temple Lane and Field entered Inner Temple as a law student, and a Lamb-Hunt meeting could have followed. Assuming a Field-Lamb acquaintance, Field may have been the nexus as late as 1811, for he contributed to the first issue of the *Reflector* while Lamb did not, and he may have suggested that Lamb contribute to the next issue. The fact that Lamb's first *Reflector* essay follows one by Field in the second issue may be significant.

George Dyer was another who knew both Lamb and Hunt during the pre-*Reflector* period. Dyer had known Lamb since at least 1796, when Lamb mentions him in a letter to Coleridge. He knew Hunt in 1808 because Hunt imitated his halting speech mannerisms in a letter to Marianne dated November 14, 1808. If Dyer was the connection between Lamb and Hunt, that association could have begun any time from 1808 on, but again there is no tangible evidence of such a beginning.

Henry Crabb Robinson may have brought Lamb and Hunt together, but this possibility is also dependent upon conjecture. We know that Robinson met Lamb in 1806 but there is no indication as to when he met Hunt. He probably knew Barron Field from 1808-1809, the years that Robinson was the editor of the *Times,* because Field was a reporter for the same paper. He

[5] In the first edition, p. xv; in the second, p. xviii.

may have known Hunt through Field, the Aikins, or any number of mutual acquaintances. Robinson's diary begins on January 1, 1811, and the first mention of Hunt is also the earliest mention anywhere of a meeting between Hunt and Lamb, January 17, 1812, just two months before the final issue of the *Reflector* came out.

> At 10 went to Barron Field's. C. Lamb, and Leigh Hunt and Mrs. Hills there. Lamb and Hunt, I found, had had a contest about Coleridge. H. had spoken of him as a bad writer, L. as of the first man he ever knew. This dispute was revived by me, but nothing remarkable was said.[6]

It seems to be a safe assumption that this was not the first time that Lamb and Hunt had met.

Lamb himself does not tell us when he and Hunt met, although he does mention it as having been brought about by chance. In his "Letter of Elia to Robert Southey" (1823) he wrote, "Accident introduced me to the acquaintance of Mr. L. H. – and the experience of his many friendly qualities confirmed a friendship between us."[7] Unfortunately the extant Lamb correspondence for the *Reflector* period is very skimpy and does not mention the *Reflector,* but writing the fourteen essays probably left little time for correspondence.

The fact that Lamb did not contribute to the first issue of the *Reflector* is strong (but circumstantial) evidence that he was not acquainted with Hunt. Had they known each other, he would have been aware that the quarterly was projected and would have been invited to contribute; one wonders if he did not see a copy of the Prospectus sometime during the summer of 1810. Since Lamb was always in need of money, he would have been eager to contribute – his fourteen items in the three issues should be sufficient evidence of eagerness. Therefore, the strong possibility exists that Lamb and Hunt were unacquainted until early in 1811, probably soon after the first issue came out, for by the time the second number was issued, in July, Lamb had rounded

[6] *Life*, I, 437.

[7] *London Magazine* for October 1823; in *The Works of Charles and Mary Lamb*, ed. E. V. Lucas (London, 1903), I, 232.

up three personal essays and a short miscellaneous piece for it. Field may have suggested that he contribute or suggested that Hunt invite his contributions. Then, too, it is possible that after Lamb saw the first issue, he recognized the *Reflector* as an outlet for his material and as a source of much-needed revenue. It seems doubly strange that neither Charles nor Mary mentioned the magazine in their letters, few as they are, because it must have meant a comfortable increase in income for them.

Hunt's harsh treatment of Wordsworth in "The Feast of the Poets" in the fourth *Reflector* is another indication that the Lamb-Hunt acquaintance was not of long standing, for if it had been, Lamb's appreciation for Wordsworth's poetry would have influenced Hunt, and he would not have written in his *Autobiography* that he was not acquainted with Wordsworth's poetry when he wrote the poem. Lucas says that, although the Lambs visited Hunt frequently in Surrey Gaol, he "was not at that time, if ever, a very intimate friend",[8] and this was two years after Lamb and Hunt were certainly acquainted.

Thus it would appear that, while Lamb and Hunt could have been acquainted as early as 1801 or 1804 through Field, by 1808 through Dyer, or almost any time after 1806 through Robinson, the logical conclusion remains that their friendship began early in 1811 and the *Reflector* brought them together.

Whatever the "accident" that introduced Lamb to Hunt, the short-term results in the *Reflector* and the long-term results to the essay genre are benefits for which the world can indeed be grateful. If Lamb's literary production could be plotted on a graph, the line would show an inverted V for 1811, an abrupt rise with just as abrupt a falling off in the following year, for, with the exception of his occasional writing for the *Examiner,* he published only three essays during the next eight years. This bulge of productivity coincidental with the *Reflector* years is ample evidence of the *Reflector*'s beneficent effect on Lamb, and in spite of the futility of considering might-have-been's, the world is the poorer for the cessation of that magazine. On the other hand, Lamb may have about written himself out in that burst of

8 *Life,* I, 453.

production, and the fallow period which followed was necessary for the more abundant harvest which was to follow – the Elia essays. Much has been written about the happy circumstances which presumably surrounded Lamb's relations with the *Reflector,* the unrestricted freedom which permitted Lamb and the essay to develop and to become a way-station en route to the fully developed familiar essay of a decade later, but Lucas expresses it as well as any:

> The *Reflector* gave Lamb his first encouragement to spread his wings with some of the freedom that an essayist demands. He did not make the fullest use of it; he was not yet ready to be the chartered egotist that he afterwards became: diffidence, humility, mistrust, stood in his way; but it is not too much to say that had he lacked the preliminary training which his *Reflector* exercises gave him, his *Elia* essays would have been the poorer. One indeed of the *Reflector* pieces afterwards became an *Elia* essay – the "Bachelor's Complaint of the Behaviour of Married People"; while the fine critical acumen displayed in two of the *Reflector* essays, those upon Hogarth and Shakespeare's Tragedies, was never excelled in his later writings.[9]

Lamb is not represented in the first issue of the *Reflector*, but he made up for lost time in the remaining issues, with ninety-three pages of material consisting of two long critical essays, a poem, and a dozen essays of various types and lengths. All of this material was not produced in 1811: the poem dates back to 1805, the circumstances of two of the essays come from previous years, and the germ of the Hogarth essay probably had its beginning early in the decade, but this still leaves a formidable record for the year. Lamb's inspiration can be traced to his reading, his experiences, his occupation, and his fertile imagination; but we recognize in him something of the same power that he saw in Shakespeare, a power that creates, through the "indigenous faculties of our minds . . . a full and clear echo" of his own (II, 304). While the critical essays have stood the test of time and are considered among Lamb's best writings from the standpoint of perception and technique, the other essays are largely conventional in form, following the path set by the eighteenth century, but deeply infused with Lamb's personality with all of its twinkling

[9] *Ibid.*, I, 417-418.

humor and its occasional paradox. They were preliminary training for Elia.

All but one of the fourteen *Reflector* items by Lamb are credited to him in the British Museum copy and all have been reprinted in various editions of his works. Lamb thought enough of nine of the essays to include them in his *Works* (1818) and even include two under the section "Letters Under Assumed Signatures, Published in 'The Reflector'" which did not belong there.[10] The poem is signed "C. Lamb" while the "assumed signatures" on the essays are various: the familiar names of fictitious correspondents, such as L, LB, X, Y, XYZ, and Crito, and Latin words suitable to particular papers, such as Pensilis, Moriturus, and Innuptus. Only one literary genre in which Lamb wrote is not represented in the *Reflector*, the drama; the essays do show Lamb as a critic, as an antiquarian, as a poet, and as a periodical essayist with a firm background in the essays of Addison and Steele.

Lamb's justly famous essays on Hogarth and Shakespeare are his only critical articles in the *Reflector*. Though his mastery of the familiar essay was not to come for another decade, these essays show that he already possessed a well-developed technique and mastery of method for the critical essay.[11] They are longer than the personal essays, as is usual with persuasive writing, and both have the subjectivity of a personal expression combined with the objectivity of a reasoned and reasonable argument.

The starting points of the critical essays are ostensibly personal experiences that initiate a train of thought, with the author's literary background, feelings, and personal responses comprising material which has the stamp of one personality but an almost universal viewpoint. In this respect the essays resemble the personal essay of the eighteenth century. Lamb's own responses of sympathy, amazement, or passion are stated with a tacit assumption of their validity. The first person, though not emphasized,

10 "The Londoner" from the *Morning Post*, February 1, 1802, and "On the Melancholy of Tailors" from *The Champion*, December 4, 1814.
11 Watson, p. 80.

is yet pervasive, but the factual statement, quotations, and reasons give the essays the objectivity that takes them out of the limited realm of opinion, standing on facts rather than the force of a personality. In both essays Lamb anticipates and meets contradiction, building up a credible position and stating his contentions unequivocally.

Wordsworthian Romanticism is reflected in these essays, with emphasis on the importance and the trustworthiness of the imagination and its responses to the paintings and plays. Appreciation for the lower-class subjects in the Hogarths, the attention paid to the characters of Shakespeare, the sympathy and emotion so prominent in both essays – all are parts of the fabric of Romanticism. The chatty style of a personal essay is lacking, but the ease of expression, the art that conceals art, prevents stylization or stereotype. Lamb avoided his characteristic puns but occasionally indulged in alliteration, with one sentence containing no less than ten examples. But in their reason, logic, and conviction the essays have lived as fine examples of their kind, and while one would not expect "Theatralia" to influence the reading or performing of Shakespeare's plays, the Hogarth essay has exercised a continuing influence on the taste and appreciation of successive generations.

Volume II, Number 3: "On the Genius and Character of Hogarth; with Some Remarks on a Passage in the Writings of the Late Mr. Barry." (Signed "L")

In his *Diary* entry for July 28, 1811, Henry Crabb Robinson recorded a conversation in which Coleridge "praised warmly an essay on Hogarth by C. Lamb, and spoke of *wrongers* of subjects as well as *writers* on them".[12] Three months later that essay was published in the third *Reflector* (II, 61-77). It had a long gestation period in Lamb's mind, for as he says in the first line, "One of the earliest and noblest enjoyments I had when a boy was in the contemplation of those capital prints by Hogarth, the *Harlot's*

[12] *Diary, Reminiscences, and Correspondence of Henry Crabb Robinson*, ed. Thomas Sadler (Boston, 1869), I, 217.

and *Rake's Progresses,* which, along with some others, hung upon the walls of a great hall in an old-fashioned house in –shire" (II, 61). This early pleasure and appreciation remained with Lamb throughout his life, and the prints which adorned his walls were conversation pieces at his Wednesday and Thursday "evenings" and in his letters. Talfourd, describing an evening at the Lamb apartment in Inner Temple Lane, wrote that "the Hogarths, in narrow black frames, abounding in infinite thought, humour and pathos, enrich the walls; and all things wear an air of comfort and hearty English welcome".[13] When Lamb described his rooms in a letter to Manning, he remembered his Hogarths: "In my best room is a choice collection of the works of Hogarth, an English painter of some humour." [14] In their rooms over an ironmonger's on Great Russell Street, with Drury Lane across from them and Covent Garden Theatre behind them, where they moved in 1817, the Lambs removed the Hogarths from their frames and bound them in a book so that Mary could examine them more closely through her spectacles. As to the essay, Coleridge was not the only one who appreciated it; Robinson mentions it about a week after it was published: "Lamb's very fine essay on Hogarth which I had read before with great delight".[15]

The Hogarth essay has been reprinted many times, in literary anthologies and in books on Hogarth. Nichols and Steevens printed it in *The Works of Hogarth* in 1817, with the following introductory paragraph:

> The following ingenious Essay was originally printed in *The Reflector*, No. iii, 1811, and is here copied by the express permission of Mr. Leigh Hunt, the Organ and principal Proprietor of the interesting Periodical Publication; on whose authority I thus make my acknowledgments to Mr. Charles Lamb, of the India House, the elegant Author of the Essay.[16]

In 1818 Lamb included the essay in his *Works*. In 1833 it appeared in a new edition of Trusler's *The Works of William*

13 *Life,* I, 512.
14 *Letters,* II, 89.
15 *Life,* I, 431.
16 *Works,* I, 48.

Hogarth and in *Anecdotes of William Hogarth* edited by John Bowyer Nichols. Appreciation for the essay has continued, and it is one of the two essays on which Lamb's reputation as a critic was founded and has remained.

Lamb's purpose in writing the Hogarth essay was to defend the morality of Hogarth's pictures and to counteract the assertions of the connoisseurs of his day that low life is inferior. After the Lambs returned to London from their 1809 vacation in Wiltshire, Lamb wrote to Coleridge, "We came back to our Hogarth Room", adding "I have made several acquisitions since you saw them".[17] Lucas is of the opinion that Lamb began the Hogarth essay about this time,[18] and he is probably right, but he does not indicate that it had its inception in Lamb's reading of *The Works and Life of Barry, Esq., Historical Painter*, published in 1809 and reviewed the next year by Richard Payne Knight in the *Edinburgh Review*. Half-way through the essay Lamb suddenly pauses to say, "I had written thus far, when I met with a passage in the writings of the late Mr. Barry, which, as it falls in with the *vulgar notion* respecting Hogarth, which this Essay has been employed in combating, I shall take the liberty to transcribe" (II, 70). By "vulgar notion" Lamb could mean either "popular opinion" or "the notion that Hogarth's pictures are vulgar". But his statement is a fiction, a device for introducing the quotation from Barry, for the preceding pages of the essay consisted of a refutation of two of Barry's points and use almost his exact words: Barry had expressed an opinion of Bunbury, the caricaturist (who died in 1811), and asserted that "Hogarth's general aim is only to shake the sides" (II, 71). While the general idea of Hogarth's excellence had been in Lamb's mind for many years and the article is an exposition of that excellence, the motivation for the essay lies in his defense against Barry's superficial and condescending observations and against the popular notion that an artist who paints low life must therefore be vulgar himself, or at least immoral. But Lamb says that "The quantity of thought which Hogarth crowds into every picture would alone unvulgarize every subject which he might

[17] *Letters*, II, 83.
[18] *Life*, I, 404.

choose" (II, 64). *Gin Lane*, for example, conveys the very practical lesson that dissipation leads to ruin. The pictures are effective because they "have the teeming, fruitful, suggesting meaning of *words*. Other pictures we look at, – his prints we read" (II, 61-62). Lamb observes an affinity between Shakespeare and Hogarth, equating the final scene in the *Rake's Progress* with a scene in *King Lear* and the Rake's story and moral with *Timon of Athens*. Using a favorite expression of Hunt's, Lamb says that "Hogarth has impressed a *thinking character* upon the persons of his canvas", giving his pictures "matter for the mind of the beholder to feed on for the hour together" (II, 66), for Hogarth is so much more than "a mere comic painter, as one whose chief ambition was to *raise a laugh*" (II, 61). He says that the pictures are Juvenalian satires, and even those which are intentionally comical do more than excite mirth: "We are led into long trains of reflection by them. In this respect they resemble the characters of Chaucer's Pilgrims"; both Hogarth and Chaucer could crowd "into one small canvas so many diverse yet cooperating materials" (II, 68).

Though Hogarth lived a generation or more prior to the appearance of the "Preface" to the *Lyrical Ballads*, his affinity to the ideas of the Romantic period is evident, and it comes as no surprise that Lamb was "indulging all my life a passion for the works of this artist" (II, 75). Lamb's essay reflects his own innate capacity for sympathy in his ability to respond to the "low" subjects of Hogarth with understanding rather than repugnance. The pictures "appeal . . . first and foremost to the very heart of man, its best and most serious feelings" (II, 61), he wrote, and Hogarth's imagination, much like Shakespeare's, is "that power which draws all things to one, which makes things animate and inanimate" (II, 64), with realism that is close to nature, and with depth of feeling, "the sorrowing by which the heart is made better" (II, 74). Barry insisted that, since life is short, it should be spent in pursuit of what is amiable and admirable and "gives a value and a dignity to human nature" (II, 71). Lamb's attitude is one which recognizes reality and sees value and dignity in human nature regardless of social rank. He becomes vehement over Barry's suggestion that the "delicacy" of a Mr. Penny is more admirable than the "raw and unformed" art of Hogarth: "But, good God! is this *milk for babes* to be set up in opposition to Hogarth's moral scenes, his strong meat for men?" (II, 72). Thus he finds morality in the faithful representation of life.

When Robinson read Lamb's essay to the sculptor, Flaxman, on November 4, 1811, Flaxman "acknowledged the literary merit of the piece, but he by no means concurred in the opinion that C. L. maintains that Hogarth is a moral painter. On the contrary F. asserted that he was a very wicked though witty artist".[19] Flaxman is representative of the more formal, sentimental pseudo-realism of the Historical School, headed by Sir Joshua Reynolds of the late eighteenth century, and part of the group whose opinions Lamb was trying to combat. Lamb's preference for the realism of Hogarth is part of the reaction of the early nineteenth century to that sentimental formalism and is an overt manifestation of the democratizing tendencies of those years of struggle with Napoleon and of agitation for reform. The "democratic" realism of Hogarth went hand in hand with other liberal elements of the time, such as the increase in humanitarian work, the abolition of slavery, and the modification of penal laws. Lamb's essay helped to focus attention on Hogarth and the liberal tendencies. If any vindication of Lamb's essay is needed, it is the better appreciation of Hogarth which was evident in 1814 when the British Institution held an exhibition of Hogarth's pictures. Richard Payne Knight, whose 1810 *Edinburgh Review* articles showed him to be no great admirer of Barry, wrote the catalog for the exhibition, stressing not only the morality of the pictures, but the technical skill as well.[20] Thus Lamb's essay contributed to the growing appreciation of Hogarth which in turn reflected the democratic trend of the times; at the same time it applied the Wordsworthian dictum for common language to the visual arts.

19 *Life*, I, 431.

20 Frederick Antal, *Hogarth and His Place in European Art* (London, 1962), p. 187.

Volume II, Number 4: "Theatralia, No. 1. – On Garrick, and Acting, and the Plays of Shakespeare, Considered with Reference to their Fitness for Stage Representation." (Signed "X")

Lamb's Shakespeare essay in the *Reflector* (II, 298-313) was to have been the first of a series in that declining medium, the essay serial. Besides having the general title of "Theatralia, No. 1.", the essay concluded with the statement that the author would extend his thesis "in some future Number" to the comedies as being "equally incompatible with stage representation" (II, 313). However, the discontinuance of the *Reflector* seems to have stemmed this flow of inspiration. When the essay was reprinted in the *Works* of 1818, the title became "On the Tragedies of Shakespeare, Considered with Reference to their Fitness for Stage Representation", thereby eliminating the emphasis on Garrick, and the essay has appeared under the revised title from that time. Lamb also modified the last paragraph to remove the reference to future numbers.

Probably this essay too had some of its inception in Lamb's Wednesday evening gatherings where its thesis could be proposed, developed, and defended in the witty and unrestrained interplay of ideas. Barnes told Lamb, "You have written about Shakespeare's own Lear, finer than any one ever did in the world",[21] and while his contemporaries no doubt agreed on this point, some of them disagreed with the thesis. Coleridge, a frequent visitor at the Lambs' and with whom Lamb had discussed the subject, expressed the opinion in one of his 1811 lectures that Shakespeare's plays are to be read but not acted, while Godwin said that the plays are so well fitted for performance that they are the only ones that deserve to be performed.[22]

Actually Lamb does not assert that the plays of Shakespeare should not be performed, but that the plays lose something in the performance, that the reading experience reveals greater

21 *Life*, I, 439.
22 *Diary*, I, 227, entry for December 15, 1811.

depth and furnishes more satisfaction than the viewing. Characteristically, Lamb begins the essay with a personal experience, "a turn the other day in the Abbey", when he noticed for the first time a monument which had been there for around twenty years, the "harlequin figure" of Garrick. Its presence there seemed incongruous to him, but what particularly aroused his indignation was the "farrago of false thoughts and nonsense" expressed in the lines on its base (II, 299). The attribution of equal talent to playwright and actor brought a marvel that anyone could confuse the "low tricks" of the actor with the poet's ability to originate "poetical images". When one goes to a play, he experiences a distinct pleasure in seeing one's conceptions embodied and realized on the stage, but this materialization is actually the substituting of a substance for a "fine vision", and only those plays which have not been seen in performance retain a "delightful sensation of freshness" for the reader. Lamb contends that "the plays of Shakespeare are less calculated for performance on a stage, than those of almost any other dramatist whatever" (II, 300). That is, Shakespeare's plays become another thing by being acted, suffering a change in the translation from page to stage and losing much in the process because Shakespeare's characters "are so much the objects of meditation rather than of interest or curiosity as to their actions". Rather than their actions, we consider "the ambition, the aspiring spirit, the intellectual activity" when we are reading (II, 307). When we read Lear, we become Lear, whereas in seeing him on the stage "we want to take him into shelter and relieve him" (II, 308). This is an instance wherein "the sight actually destroys the faith", because "the reading of a tragedy is a fine abstraction" (II, 310, 312). When we see a play, we become judges and critics and change our attitude toward it, just as a reviewer approaches a fine poem more critically than one who is reading it for pleasure.

In his insistence that Shakespeare's plays are better suited to reading than performance and in his concentration upon the characters, Lamb is expressing a typically Romantic stance, that of exalting the inner man over the external, of emphasizing the function of the imagination, an attitude to which, in part at least, can be attributed the paucity of great plays and the prominence of the closet drama through much of the nineteenth century. Lamb, Barnes, and Hunt were all concerned with the living theatre, with actors and staging, with the externals, and all agreed that the reader of a play could derive a greater depth of pleasure and appreciation from it than a spectator at a performance. They do not take into account, in this assertion, that all readers would not be as responsive or perceptive as they, that some would respond more wholly to a performance than to a reading. In the preface to his *Descent of Liberty* Hunt wrote, "Who, that has any fancy at all, does not feel that he can raise much better pictures in his own mind than he finds in the theatre?" [23] Hunt's question reminds us of his low opinion of the theatre during the *Reflector* period and also that many viewers had little "fancy" and would be better viewers than readers.

The concentration on characters to the subordination of other factors is a Romantic trait which is sometimes blamed (or credited) with the increase in the closet drama in that period.[24] But in his Shakespeare essay Lamb is underscoring the dominance of the inner mind over the outer, of the imagination that informs all things, creating and transforming, so that the reading of Shakespeare is a creating experience while seeing the play is a second-hand representation on a lower level of experience. He says that many of the characters have a depth which can only be plumbed by the imagination in the "slow apprehension" of reading, that "fine vision" which the imagination permits and a performance is apt to destroy. This conclusion is reasonable, but as Ralli points out and as Shakespeare would probably have agreed, both man and the drama have a duality, the internal thought and external action as well as inner mind and outer body, and the one complements the other. "The business of art

[23] Leigh Hunt, *The Descent of Liberty, a Mask* (London, 1816), p. liii.

[24] Carl R. Woodring, however, says that this is a misinterpretation, that "Romantic study of character on stage . . . belongs not only to the reader's closet but also to the theatre." *Prose of the Romantic Period*, ed. Carl R. Woodring (Boston, 1961), p. xiv.

is to suggest, not affirm",[25] and the skill of a good actor can also be a stimulus to the imagination just as extensively as the printed word.[26]

Volume II, Number 4: "Specimens from the Writings of Fuller, the Church Historian" (Signed "Y")

From his early years in the East India House to the more leisurely times after his retirement, Lamb pursued his hobby of reading the old and half-forgotten dramatists and historians and recording excerpts from them in his Book of Extracts, as he called his commonplace book. Lamb's hobby not only provided him with publishable material for himself and his friends but also, consciously or not, influenced his individual style and diction.

Lamb's friend, Bryan Waller Procter, wrote that "Lamb's pleasures (except perhaps from his pipes) lay among the books of the old English writers. His soul delighted in communion with ancient generations; more especially, with men who had been unjustly forgotten."[27] Lamb shared this pleasure when he published his *Specimens of English Dramatic Poets,* which, though a financial failure, was the foundation of his critical reputation. As he himself pointed out, the *Specimens* aroused the interest of ordinary readers in the old dramatists.[28] When the opportunity came to write for the *Reflector,* he naturally turned to his Book of Extracts for material, as he was to do at other times: for example, in the *Indicator* in 1821, in Hone's *Every-Day Book* in 1826, and in his revised *Dramatic Specimens* in 1835. In addition, he probably furnished quotations to his friends whenever they needed them.

The *Reflector* specimens (I, 342-348) are from Thomas Fuller,

[25] Augustus Ralli, *A History of Shakespearian Criticism* (New York, 1949), I, 144.

[26] For excellent examinations of this essay, see Charles I. Peterson, Jr., "Charles Lamb, Shakespeare, and the Stage Reconsidered", *Emory University Quarterly,* XX (1964), 101-107, and John I. Ades, "Charles Lamb, Shakespeare, and Early Nineteenth-Century Theater", *PMLA*, LXXXV (May 1970), 514-526.

[27] Bryan Waller Procter, *An Autobiographical Fragment* ... (London, 1877), II, 125.

[28] *Life*, I, 398–400.

the historian and divine who lived from 1608 to 1661, and consist of thirty-nine examples from three Fuller works which Lamb read in the British Museum. Each selection has a short subject or title, but sources are not given.[29] The compilation – for this can hardly be called an essay – begins with two short paragraphs, signed "Y"; this signature and a part of the final footnote were omitted in the *Works* of 1818. Since Fuller is rarely read except by antiquaries, Lamb writes, he is presenting "some Specimens of his manner" to show that he is not just quaint but has an "eager liveliness" and "his conceits are oftentimes deeply steeped in human feeling and passion" (I, 342). Lamb's comments are continued in the footnotes. In the excerpts can be discerned Lamb's appreciation for simile and metaphor, imagination, turn of phrase, warmth of soul and generosity, a twinkle in the eye – and for the few kind words for short men. Lamb finds a similarity in style between Fuller and Sir Thomas Browne, another of his favorites. In the final footnote he says that criticism too often accentuates what a writer lacks rather than what is excellent, and to say that Fuller's only quality is quaintness is unjust.

The effect of the old writers on Lamb's literary style is difficult to pinpoint; rather, it is pervasive. His writings, even the few in the *Reflector*, abound in archaisms and allusions which are now obscure.[30] Hunt wrote, regarding the Elia essays, "Nor will they be liked the less for a sprinkle of old language, which was natural in him by reason of his great love of the old English writers."[31] Lamb, as we know him from his letters and essays, has a genuine affinity with the Fuller who is revealed in the specimens; as Hine expresses it, the garden of Lamb's muse has Fuller's earth for its topsoil.[32]

Volume I, Number 2: "On the Inconveniences Resulting from Being Hanged" (Signed "Pensilis")

[29] Lucas lists the sources in *Works*, I, 417-418.

[30] Tsutomu Kukuda, *A Study of Charles Lamb's "Essays of Elia"* (Tokyo, 1964) has two chapters on archaisms in the Essays.

[31] "Charles Lamb", in *Leigh Hunt's London Journal*, January 7, 1835.

[32] Reginald Leslie Hine, *Charles Lamb and His Hertfordshire* (London, 1949), p. 292.

"On the Danger of Confounding Moral With Personal Deformity, with a Hint to Those who Have the Framing of Advertisements for Apprehending Offenders" (Signed "Crito")

"On the Probable Effects of the Gunpowder Treason to This Country if the Conspirators Had Accomplished Their Object" (Signed "Speculator")

"On the Ambiguities Arising from Proper Names" (Signed "XYZ")

Lamb's first *Reflector* essays, the four in the second issue, are firmly grounded in the essay tradition of the eighteenth century, looking toward Addison and Steele rather than toward Elia. Only in their uniquely Lamb flavor do they anticipate his more famous essays of a decade later. They average about five pages in length, are in letter form, and with one exception have signatures which are Latin words appropriate to the personality or fortunes of the imaginary writer. None are character sketches *per se* and only the short note on proper names is an actual incident, but all have the conventional light touch, a certain amount of didacticism, and a generous sprinkling of the Lamb personality. They give the impression of a personal essay with the use of the first person and an occasional autobiographical element, but for the most part it is Lamb the dramatist at work, speaking through a persona.

It would be interesting to know just what supplied the idea for Lamb's account of Pensilis, who was hanged (I, 381-388). Executions by hanging were everyday affairs in England then, as anyone who has read newspapers of the day can testify, and while Lamb's sensitive nature would probably prevent his witnessing a hanging, periodicals could give him an abundance of verbal pictures. The essay, reprinted in the 1818 *Works,* furnished some of the particulars for Lamb's farce, *The Pawnbroker's Daughter* (1825), in which Jack Pendulus is revived after being hanged. By his manner and his actions Pensilis reveals himself to be a self-conscious, sensitive person who suffers more from his notoriety as one who has been hanged then he did in being hanged, who is the victim of the tactlessness of his friends, the jibes of his enemies, and the faithlessness of friends of both sexes. His macabre experience has made him an object of sympathy – and Lamb is always sympathetic. Paradoxically, Pensilis' complete lack of a sense of humor makes him somewhat humorous. The essay has a few Lamb trade-marks: mention of his uncle's seat in –shire, use of an incident from Shakespeare, the puns on hanging, quoting Tom Brown of Shifnal, as he does so often.

Lamb rarely injected politics into his writing. His only completely political composition is "The Triumph of the Whale", and political overtones appear in the Gunpowder Treason essay. But near the end of the Pensilis essay Lamb inserted a short phrase about whipping which the reader of 1811 would recognize and respond to. Objecting to the "barber-like ministering" and the valet-like fumbling of the hangman's hand at one's collar, Pensilis says that the guillotine would be preferable because it is an agency that functions more of itself. "In beheading, indeed, as it was formerly practiced in England, and in whipping to death, as is sometimes practiced now, the hand of man is no doubt sufficiently busy" (I, 388). Flogging was still used by the British army, but public objections to it caused it to be abandoned soon after the *Reflector* period.

The closing paragraph concerns hangmen in Germany, where (he says) their position is hereditary and marriages are common between the families of hangmen from different parishes. This fantastic notion elicited a "Letter to the Editor" published in the third *Reflector* entitled "Inquiries Respecting Jack Ketch" and speculating about that traditional hangman and his race of Ketchidae (II, 203-206).

Lamb's second *Reflector* essay (I, 424-429) is related in theme to his Hogarth essay, for it concerns man's error in attributing low morals to persons simply because they are unattractive physically. In this case, however, the error is reversed, that of describing offenders inaccurately because one is influenced by the nature of the offense. The article takes its inception from an advertisement, probably an authentic one, for a man who has jumped bail and whose description consists of many derogatory adjectives. Crito advises writers of advertisements for the apprehension of offenders that greater objectivity would result in greater accuracy in their descriptions. The essay is in letter form and has a digression near the beginning, both conventional devices used by Lamb's predecessors. Lamb's sympathetic humanity is strongly evident as are a number of typically Lamb stylistic devices, such as his predilection for the long appositive series, often ending with "&c", in this case listing the things we have read and seen which influence our preconceptions about offenders.

The essay on the Gunpowder Plot (I, 429-435) had to wait until 1823 before it was reprinted in a modified form: It was re-titled "Guy Faux", given three new paragraphs at the beginning, and published in the *London Magazine* as an Elia essay.[33] The germ of the essay is another of Lamb's "Specimens", this time a 1638 sermon by Bishop Taylor on the anniversary of the gunpowder treason incident. Taylor, he says, lived closer to the actual incident so that he could write about it in "words that burn", but time and children have made the incident almost a fable. Therefore, he feels that he will not be accused of profaning the subject if he takes a light view of it. If the plot had been successful, there would have been a drastic change in the nobility of the country, and he himself might now be a duke or an earl. This notion can also be found in a letter to Manning dated January 2, 1810, wherein he listed his titles from "Mr. C. Lamb" to "Duke Lamb", then facetiously carrying them on to King Lamb, Emperor Lamb, and "Pope Innocent, higher than which is nothing but the Lamb of God".[34] Then in his fancy he sees the House blown up, an "adjournment in the air *sine die*" (I, 434). As the MP's enter the firmament, they become constellations. A passage omitted from the 1823 version mentions two "constellations" that are of topical though lasting interest: Sir Vicary Gibbs, the attorney general, ends up next to Scorpion, while "the gentle Castlereagh curdles

[33] *London Magazine*, VIII (November, 1823), 477-481. The essay was not included in *The Essays of Elia*, however.
[34] *Letters*, II, 89-90.

in the Milky Way" (I, 434). This would be one way of eliminating corruption in Parliament, even more complete than Pride's Purge. Then he turns from fantasy to reality, urging that Parliament be changed but not wiped out, for honest Englishmen can do so with "integrity and patriotic intention" (I, 435). This is the most politically oriented of any Lamb essay, and its gentle whimsy contrasts strongly with the outspoken criticism of so many other *Reflector* essays.

The first three *Reflector* essays by Lamb were reprinted by him, and Hunt put Lamb's name on them in the British Museum copy of the *Reflector*. The fourth item (I, 484-485) was never acknowledged by Lamb, nor did Hunt put Lamb's name on it, though this is not surprising in view of its inconsequential nature. But identification is not difficult, since the item describes an incident which Lamb recounted in a letter to Wordsworth dated February 1, 1806. The one-page letter concerns the confusion which can arise when two names are pronounced alike but spelled differently, in this case the name Spenser. The letter is straight narrative; its moral would have been more forceful if Lamb had included a line from the letter to Wordsworth: "Nothing like defining of Terms when we talk."[35] The item is primarily of interest because Lamb wrote it, but it exemplifies his retention and use of past experience and thoughts in his writing. While it is well written and interesting, it is merely an anecdote, and it shows that Lamb was dipping rather deeply into the well of memory, spurred by economic necessity to something very close to hack writing.

Volume II, Number 4: "A Farewell to Tobacco" (Signed "C. Lamb")
"Edax on Appetite" (Signed "Edax")
"Hospita on the Immoderate Indulgence of the Pleasures of the Palate" (Signed "Hospita")

Whether it was by accident or by design, Lamb's three *Reflector*

[35] *Letters*, I, 420, 421.

items which have to do with his gustatory proclivities are grouped together in the final issue. "Edax on Appetite" probably suggested the companion piece, "Hospita on the Immoderate Indulgence . . .", and perhaps the two reminded Lamb of his poem on another kind of indulgence, a poem he had included in a letter to the Wordsworths in September 1805, "A Farewell to Tobacco".

Lamb was always giving up smoking and never quite succeeding. In 1803 the first expression of his doubts about tobacco appear in a letter to Coleridge: "Maybe the truth is, that *one* pipe is wholesome, *two* pipes toothsome, *three* pipes noisome, *four* pipes fulsome, *five* pipes quarrelsome; and that's the sum on't. But that is deciding rather upon rhyme than reason." [36] Lamb wrote "A Farewell to Tobacco" sometime in 1805, the only product of a long period of inactivity; as he wrote to Wordsworth, "But now I have bid farewell to my 'Sweet Enemy' Tobacco . . . I perhaps shall set soberly to work." [37] In the poem he says that he is giving up tobacco on his physician's orders, but the separation was only temporary. He was still giving up smoking the following March when he wrote to Hazlitt, "I, going to leave off smoke. In mean time am so smoky with last night's 10 Pipes, that I must leave off." [38]

The poem (II, 387-391) is one of the two items in the four issues of the *Reflector* which have the authors' names appended to them. In it he extolls tobacco, "Brother of Bacchus", as something for which he "would do anything but die". As Lamb describes it in his letter to Wordsworth, the poem is "a little in the way of Withers", bouncing tetrameter couplets with some off-rhymes and double-rhymes. Lamb made some minor revisions when he reprinted the poem in his *Works*. One line is of special significance: "For I hate, yet love thee so", expressing the closeness between love and hate and again pointing to the combinations of opposites in human nature, of good and bad, the morality which appears so often in Lamb's writings and attitudes.

[36] *Ibid.*, I, 345.
[37] *Ibid.*, I, 401.
[38] *Ibid.*, I, 424.

The Edax and Hospita essays are a unique pair, showing Lamb's ability to project himself into personae not only of different temperaments but of both sexes. Edax, the glutton, is a compulsive eater, and the account of his gargantuan appetite is amusing yet pitiful, arousing sympathy and a little repugnance – the duality of man's nature again. Though he uses the first person, the essays are not autobiographical; even the clergyman father whom he mentions is imaginary. But the personal essayist feels no obligation to be true to his own biography, for his façade, his imaginary self, permits him to be anything his imagination can contrive. Thus this matching pair resembles two dramatic monologues giving different viewpoints of a single situation.

The Edax essay (II, 391-397) begins very much like the one by Pensilis, with the dashes, the suspense, the exaggeration, and the bursting forth of the shocking revelation. Other stylistic devices characteristic of Lamb are the appositive series, the implied pun on his name, the fun with words. This persona is more literate than Pensilis, for he can quote appropriate excerpts from Horace, Pliny, Pope, and that old Lamb favorite, Mandeville. Lamb makes his moral very explicit at the end of the essay: A plea for understanding of his compulsive eating because "an original peculiarity of constitution is no crime", and "Not that which goes into the mouth desecrates man, but that which comes out of it" (II, 397).

In the companion piece (II, 397-399), Hospita complains about a friend of her husband's whose failing is "an immoderate indulgence of his palate", and even without the editor's footnote (omitted when reprinting) we realize that she is talking about Edax. The essay becomes Lamb's sole excursion into economics when he mentions the food shortage and Malthus' "Thoughts on the Ratio of Food to Population". Both the Edax and the Hospita essays are closely related to "A Bachelor's Complaint" in the resemblances between Edax and the bachelor, between Hospita and the wives of the bachelor's friends, and in their general incompatibility. Certainly the reader's sympathies are with the bachelor in both cases, just as Lamb's sympathy and understanding were with an actual bachelor, George Dyer. And Lamb could speak of bachelors from personal experience, for he was one, too.

Volume II, Number 3: "On Burial Societies: and the Character of an Undertaker" (Signed "Moriturus")

"On the Custom of Hissing at the Theatres, with Some Account of a Club of Damned Authors" (Signed "Semel-Damnatus")

Volume II, Number 4: "A Bachelor's Complaint of the Behaviour of Married People" (Signed "Innuptus")

"The Good Clerk, a Character; with Some Account of *The Complete English Tradesman*" (Signed "LB")

Both "On Burial Societies" and "The Good Clerk" have within them sketches in the manner of the seventeenth century character writers, Hall, Overbury, and Fuller. The "Character of an Undertaker" is the concluding section of "Burial Societies", while the sketch of the Clerk is the first part of the other essay. In the Theophrastian manner these sketches describe a type rather than a particular person, and the orientation of both essays is toward the past.

"On Burial Societies" (II, 140-144) begins as a traditional essay, using, as did the essay on personal deformity, an advertisement as a central element. "Moriturus", the persona, has been given a handbill advertising a burial society, and in its intriguing details he finds a stimulus for his imagination and a basis for his puns and wit. The remainder of the essay is somewhat of a digression. He uses the old device of finding a manuscript among the effects of a departed friend (the same device used by Barnes in his Belles and Beaux essay of the fourth *Reflector*), and this manuscript, a Theophrastian "character" describing an undertaker, concludes the essay. The subject of death and matters related to it appeared occasionally in eighteenth century essays but rarely in the light-hearted manner of Lamb. The letter form, the "discovery" of the paper, the "character", the biographical beginning, and the personal experience are all conventional. The essay was reprinted in part in *The Yellow Dwarf* for January 17, 1818, and also in the 1818 *Works*.

"The Good Clerk" (II, 432-437) is one of the few *Reflector* essays by Lamb not in the pseudo-epistolary form. Though it was not reprinted by Lamb, the essay was used by William Hone in his *Table Book* (1837) in a somewhat modified form, and signed "L".

Lamb's essay reflects a combination of observation and reading, of his use of experience and his interest in literature of the past. In describing his generalized clerk, Lamb seems to be seated at his desk at the East India House, letting his eyes move with sympathetic perception from one to another of his fellow clerks and letting his pen record their characteristics in a composite picture. Lamb was about thirty-six at the time, neither the youngest nor the oldest of the clerks; he could observe both ages with objectivity and recognize in the older clerks a dedication to the routine which was to become so unbearable to Lamb as he reached retirement age. Apparently the primary aim of a good clerk is to please his employers, even relegating such qualities as Christianity and patriotism to less important stations. He is representative of maxims of a century ago, so Lamb describes him in archaic diction: "He writeth a fair and clear hand" (II, 432). While the Theophrastian mode of the first part of the essay goes back to the seventeenth century, the content of the second part goes back to Defoe, whose *Complete English Tradesman* puzzles Lamb. He cannot decide if Defoe is serious or if he has written a "covered satire", for he cannot conceive of a merchant's completely sublimating his feelings and pride in deference to inconsiderate and impertinent shoppers any more than he can the good clerk's total dedication to his job. Very likely the reading of Defoe had started a train of thought in Lamb's mind and he quickly saw the relationship between the tradesman and the devoted clerk, and both are a marvel to him.

Lamb's essay on the custom of hissing at theatres (II, 122-127) continues the traditional mode in its epistolary form with pseudonymous signature, the first-person narration of a personal experience, the comments on manners, the humor and the exaggeration – all characteristic of the eighteenth century essay. The style is typical of Lamb, with the usual appositive series, the similes, the literary allusions. Over the whole Lamb spreads a Pagliacci quality from his own individual style and personality, telling of a disappointment with a wry humor that only partly hides the pain beneath.

The essay is an outgrowth of a disappointing experience. In 1806 Lamb wrote a farce, *Mr. H.,* hoping to make some money with it. But the play failed so miserably that Lamb joined in the hissing, as he said later, so that he would not be taken for the author.[39] In a letter to his friend Manning he wrote about his "cursed fall from off the top of Drury-Lane Theatre into the pit",[40] and much of that paragraph found its way into the 1811 essay in the *Reflector*. In the essay Lamb writes that he was less disturbed by the condemnation of his play than by the manner in which it was done, that it is a pity "the sweet human voice" should be used to make noises like "silly geese, and irrational venomous snakes" (II, 123). He lists the several varieties of snakes that correspond to the spectators in the theatre and is reminded of the experience of Satan, in *Paradise Lost*, who also heard "a dismal universal hiss, the sound/ Of public scorn". He suggests that being placed in a pillory would be a less painful punishment for authors than the humiliation of being hissed – a reminder of the story of his own experience in the stocks in 1809. The second part of the essay is an account of a club of "damned

[39] *Mr. H.* was performed only once, on December 10, 1806, with Elliston playing the title role. The plot centers around the mystery of Mr. H's name; the revelation that "H" is for "Hogsflesh" and the man's decision to change his name to Bacon brought hisses which drowned out the applause of Lamb's many friends in the audience. In a different milieu the play was a success. It was performed in New York the following March and played for a number of years in Philadelphia, where it was published in 1813. In England the play was first published in Lamb's *Works* (1818).

[40] *Letters*, II, 49.

authors" to which the writer belongs and from which he derives his pseudonym of Semel-Damnatus, or "once-damned". The club consists of fourteen authors, all of whom have had one play condemned by the public; anyone who has failed twice is black-balled, for "Simple damnation we hold to be a merit, but to be twice-damned we adjudge infamous" (II, 127).

While the essay on hissing evokes feelings of sympathy and admiration in the reader, it also communicates some of the same defensive attitude which comes out in "A Bachelor's Complaint of the Behaviour of Married People" (II, 349-339A). Most bachelors feel an identification with Lamb when they read this essay, for it tells of a universal experience of bachelors in their relations with married friends. As usual in Lamb's essays, the reader finds it difficult to tell what is Lamb and what is persona, where autobiography ends and fancy begins. Many of his friends were unmarried at this time, but his relations with married friends were always cordial. The beginning of the essay is very conventional: "I am a single man not quite turned of forty, who have spent a good deal of my time in noting down the infirmities of Married People" (II, 349). They are too loving, he complains, for they parade their complacency about the married state before him in order to impress him with his less felicitous situation, putting on airs "founded on the ignorance of us unmarried people" (II, 350). When a friend marries, the friendship is certain to diminish, for wives have many subtle ways "to insult and worm you out of their husband's confidence" (II, 353). But all this is nothing compared to "the airs which these creatures give themselves when they come, as they generally do, to have children", even though the feat is no unusual accomplishment, for "the poorest people commonly have them in most abundance" (II, 351). When Lamb says "I was always rather squeamish in my women and children" or speaks of children as "brats", he gives the impression that he does not care for children; actually he had an unsentimental regard for them, considering them on their own qualities, as he did adults: "They stand with me upon their own stock, as much as men and women do" (II, 352). Parents, not children, are the objects of the impatience of Innuptus. Anyone who has shared the loving nostalgia of "Dream Children" knows Lamb's sympathy and understanding for children.

"A Bachelor's Complaint" is a conventional essay in many ways. It is a letter with a pseudonymous signature, it seems to be based on experience, and it criticizes manners and morals. After it concludes with the threat to reveal the true names of his married friends, he adds a hasty postscript to the editor: "I hope you are not a married man" (II, 339). The essay was omitted from the *Works* but was republished, without the letter form or postscript, as an essay of Elia in the *London Magazine* in 1822. Lucas says that this essay is "the earliest of the Elia essays",[41] though it was written ten years before the others, and evidently Lamb looked on it in the same way. Thus "A Bachelor's Complaint" is a specific link between the Reflector and the Elia essays, a concrete example of the importance of the *Reflector* in the development of Lamb and the familiar essay.

A study of Lamb's life and work in the year of the *Reflector* leads to three general conclusions: That Lamb's motive for writing was largely economic; that without the remuneration the *Reflector* afforded, many of his essays would never have been written; and that the opportunity to practice and experiment on the personal essay in the *Reflector* prepared Lamb for the later fully-developed familiar essay.

Lamb was always anxious to augment his East India House salary, so that the associations with the *Reflector* in 1811 and with the *London Magazine* in 1820 resulted in great bursts of literary activity by him, the two most highly productive times of his life. Both magazines paid well, and in both cases Lamb could contribute all he could write. Under such pleasant circumstances any writer would be productive, and Lamb's response to the opportunity to try his wings came from the prods of necessity as well as from the instinct to fly.

Lamb wrote or completed thirteen items during the twelve months with the *Reflector* (the "Tobacco" poem was written pre-

[41] *Works*, II, 391.

viously), though the item on the ambiguity of names is trivial and the specimens of Fuller a compilation rather than an original work. The remaining eleven items are essays of merit which must have taken considerable time to bring to a finished state, and Lamb had little spare time available to him. He was a careful craftsman, giving minute attention to detail and making extensive revisions,[42] yet his production for the period is remarkable. Since no proof exists that some of the essays were written before 1811, it follows that, if Hunt had never put out the *Reflector*, some of the thirteen items would never have been written. If the *Reflector* had continued, who knows what a wealth of critical and personal essays it would have drawn from Lamb during the next several years. Sometime after the demise of the *Reflector*, Lamb planned a two-volume edition of his essays, using the *Reflector* papers and writing new ones, but the plan was scotched by Gifford, "whom Lamb damned eternally for his interference".[43]

Not only would Lamb have been poorer without the *Reflector*, the *Reflector* would have been considerably poorer without Lamb's contributions, for to them it owes most of its fame. The critical and personal essays of Lamb in the *Reflector* are of sufficient value and importance to perpetuate the reputation of the magazine.

Lucas has remarked that "The world owes a great debt to Leigh Hunt for discerning Lamb's gifts and allowing him free reign",[44] but in view of Hunt's failure to praise Lamb in the paragraph added to the second binding of *Reflectors*, one wonders if he fully appreciated Lamb's gifts in 1811 and 1812. Up to 1811 Lamb was known primarily as a critic, for since he wrote "The Londoner" in 1802, he had no opportunity to attempt the personal essay. The *Reflector* essays are a kind of half-way station along Lamb's journey to the familiar essay. Although he had unrestricted freedom, Lamb kept his *Reflector* essays almost completely traditional, using the letter form, exaggeration, literary

42 George L. Barnett, *Charles Lamb: The Evolution of Elia* (Bloomington, 1964), p. 160 ff.

43 *Ibid.*, p. 41.

44 *Works*, I, 404.

allusions, some didacticism, and other conventions of the eighteenth century, plus, of course, much of his own style. Most innovation has its foundation in the traditional, and Lamb in 1811 was getting the training he needed before advancing to the intimacy and the bitter-sweet reminiscences of the Elia essays. He was already in his late thirties, but he needed greater maturity, more of the self-confidence that approaches egotism, which was to develop over the next eight years. Without the freedom – and the economic motivation – of the *Reflector*, Elia might never have been born.

IV

THE HUNT CIRCLE AND ITS CONTRIBUTIONS

Because some of the contributors to the *Reflector* were close friends of Hunt, the magazine has sometimes been looked upon as the product of a coterie or of a group of alumni of Christ's Hospital. Actually only four of the writers were close friends and only three of these were old Bluecoat boys; Lamb cannot be included in this group since the Lamb-Hunt connection did not begin until after the magazine was launched. Hunt knew Barnes, Mitchell, and Scholcfield when they were in school together; Barron Field joined the Hunt circle some time later. In their early interests Barnes and Field were journalists and law students; Mitchell and Scholefield were students of the classics. All four were loyal friends who were willing to assist Hunt with his new magazine.

A. THOMAS BARNES

With the exceptions of Lamb and Hunt, Thomas Barnes is the only contributor to the *Reflector* on whom there has been any recent scholarship.[1] As the distinguished editor of the *Times* from 1817 to 1841, Barnes became somewhat of a legend during his lifetime. The merging of his strong personality with a prominent newspaper made Barnes one of the most powerful men of his day. His editorship covered the years of the reform movement and its success, and he supported it wholeheartedly. He was not

[1] Derek Hudson, *Thomas Barnes of The Times* (Cambridge, 1944); *The History of the Times: The Thunderer in the Making, 1785-1841* (New York, 1935).

only a product of his times but a leading formulator of and participant in the issues and trends, and in this participation Barnes lived a full life in his fifty-five years.

Little is known of Barnes' early life. His father, John Barnes, was an attorney and a former Bluecoat Boy. Thomas Barnes was born on September 16, 1785, and on March 18, 1796, he was admitted to Christ's Hospital, where he remained until 1804, thus being a schoolmate of Hunt for about four years, of Mitchell and Scholefield for longer periods. According to Hunt, Barnes was a good scholar but less zealous than Mitchell. In 1804 Barnes went to Pembroke College, Cambridge, where he was known for his good looks, his athletic skill, and his scholarship, doing so well in Latin that he attracted the attention of the Professor of Greek, Richard Porson. He received his degree in 1808, then returned intermittently, receiving his M.A. in 1811. In London Barnes gravitated toward his old Christ's Hospital friends, renewing his friendship with Hunt and becoming a part of the group, with Hunt, at the home of Thomas Hill of the *Monthly Mirror*. Hunt is probably the one who introduced him to Barron Field, the drama critic for the *Times*, thus beginning the chain of circumstances which were to decide Barnes' career. He was still looking around late in 1808, though, and on November 11, 1808, he emulated Field by becoming a law student at the Inner Temple. The next year Field introduced Barnes to John Walter II of the *Times* as a likely prospect as a reporter (and probably as one in need of a job). When pressure of legal studies forced Field to give up some of his reporting, Barnes took over as the regular theatrical reporter, moving to the parliamentary reporting staff in January 1811. Crabb Robinson, who was also connected with the *Times* before he made law his profession, reported seeing Barnes at Lamb's on March 16, 1812, describing him in complimentary terms and as a candidate for a fellowship at Cambridge.[2] Barnes' failure to receive this fellowship was probably the deciding factor as to his career, for he remained with the *Times* for the rest of his life.

During 1810-1812 Barnes wrote a few articles for the *Reflec-*

[2] *Diary*, I, 241.

Thomas Barnes

(Painting by Sir William Newton, 1832)
(From "The History of the Times")

tor; he further exhibited his loyalty to Hunt by his conduct before and during Hunt's imprisonment. He gave Hunt legal advice and visited him frequently in Surrey Gaol, and Hunt returned the favor in typical fashion in the form of a sonnet[3] and in the dedication of *The Descent of Liberty* in 1815. During Hunt's prison term Barnes wrote the theatrical notices for the *Examiner* plus a series called "Parliamentary Criticism", signed "Criticus", of which Hunt spoke favorably in his postscripts to the *Examiner* at the end of 1813. Most of these essays were published in book form in 1815 as *Parliamentary Portraits.* In 1814-1815 he wrote a series of portraits of authors for John Scott's *Champion*, over the signature "Strada". Other essays in the *Champion* on Kean, Leigh Hunt's poetry, and the Elgin marbles, signed "S", may also have been written by Barnes.[4]

After Barnes became the editor of the *Times* in 1817, his name appeared with less frequency in the activities of his literary acquaintances. In 1818 he was at Haydon's in company with Keats, Hazlitt (who had worked as drama critic for the *Times* the previous year), and others, but generally Barnes preferred political affairs after becoming editor, though he reviewed Mitchell's book on Aristophanes for the *Times*. His correspondence with Hunt continued, off and on, to 1836. His friendship with Hunt meant much to him and its endurance owed something to Barnes' self-restraint. He often had to hold back from giving Hunt advice because it would have offended him, and, said Barnes, "I cannot bear to lose Hunt's friendship, for there is hardly a man I love so much."[5] Hunt describes Barnes in the *Autobiography*:

> He was very handsome when young, with a profile of Grecian regularity; and was famous among us for a certain dispassionate humour, for his admiration of the works of Fielding, and for his delight, nevertheless, in pushing a narrative to its utmost, and drawing upon his stores of fancy for intensifying it; an amusement for which he possessed an understood privilege. It was painful in after-life to see his

[3] "Sonnet to T.B., Esq." dated from Hampstead, January 20, 1813, in the *Examiner* (February 14, 1813), p. 104; later titled "Quiet Evenings, to Thomas Barnes, Esq.".

[4] *The History of the Times*, p. 486.

[5] *Ibid.*, p. 192.

good looks swallowed up in corpulency, and his once handsome mouth thrusting its under lip out, and panting with asthma. I believe he was originally so well constituted in point of health and bodily feeling, that he fancied he could go on, all his life, without taking any of the usual methods to preserve his comfort. . . . Barnes wrote elegant Latin verse, a classical English style, and might assuredly have made himself a name in wit and literature, had he cared much for anything beyond his glass of wine and his Fielding.[6]

Talfourd called him "one of the soundest and most elegant scholars whom Christ's Hospital ever produced".[7] Though his contemporaries lamented his desertion of literature, Barnes probably earned greater fame with the *Times* than he would have as a man of letters. He died on May 7, 1841, after a surgical operation. In comfortable financial circumstances at the time of his death, he left money for a scholarship at Cambridge. Burial took place in Kensal Green Cemetery, where Hunt was to join him eighteen years later. The influence of Thomas Barnes on journalism and on the *Times* is inestimable, for he raised both to a position of prestige and respect.

Barnes signed most of his contributions to the *Reflector* with his initials, and five of them are credited to him in the British Museum copy of the *Reflector*. One is signed with a pseudonym.[8]

Volume I, Number 1: "On the Claims of Propertius"
"Stafford's Niobe"
Miscellaneous: "On Robert Herrick's To Julia"

Volume I, Number 2: "On Theophrastus"
Miscellaneous: "Dress and Character – A Slight Sketch"

[6] *Autobiography*, p. 105.

[7] Sir Thomas Noon Talfourd, *Final Memorials of Charles Lamb* (London, 1848), II, 179.

[8] Harold Child, in an essay in the Derek Hudson biography of Barnes, infers that another *Reflector* article is by Barnes, the one on Dr. Bentley, signed "Vindex", and obviously by a Cambridge man, but it is by Barnes' friend and Cambridge schoolmate, James Scholefield.

Volume II, Number 3: "On the Right of Dower out of Personalty" (Signed "Porcia")

Volume II, Number 4: "Project for Making Beaux and Belles Useful"

Miscellaneous: "Sapphic Verses"

The titles of Barnes' essays for the *Reflector* illustrate his interest in the classics as well as his consciousness of the living present with all its foibles. He was somewhat of a feminist, as his remarks on Stafford show, and his temperament tended toward sharp criticism which was often satirical or sarcastic. Though he was engaged in theatrical reporting at the time, he let others write on the theatre in the *Reflector*, contenting himself with occasional references which reveal his dislike for Restoration and most eighteenth century dramatists.

"On the Claims of Propertius" (I, 52-59) refutes a statement of the Italian critic, Gravina, that Propertius has novelty of expression, lyrical fancy, and a talent as fitted for elegiac subjects as for amatory poetry. Barnes asserts that Propertius' frigid verses lack delicacy and pathos, are often obscene, and have an overabundance of allusions.[9] Barnes' essay is written in the first person in the form of a letter to the editor and the diction is appropriately easy without being chatty. "On Theophrastus" (I, 409-424) is likewise critical and informative but is more formal, is not epistolary, and has less of the first person pronoun. Barnes' own translations of selections from Theophrastus and his comparison of Theophrastus and La Bruyere are interesting and valuable. The short sketch "Dress and Character" (I, 477-479), based on "Clothes make the man", whimsically attempts to set up standards of characterization based on the color or colors a person is wearing.

Barnes demonstrated his good taste in poetry as well as his skill in writing Latin verse in two short items. In the first issue

[9] Eleven years later a long answer to Barnes' criticism appeared in the *London Magazine*, VI (August 1822), 125-132. Entitled "Defense of the Claims of Propertius" and signed "An Idler", it asserted that Propertius may be caustic, indignant, and acrimonious, but never frigid.

appeared his Latin translation of Robert Herrick's little poem, "The Night Piece" (I, 242-244), which he calls his "copper substitute" for Herrick's "pure gold"; he points out that while Herrick took the idea for the poem from an elegy of Propertius, the "sweetness and tenderness to be found in it . . . are the exclusive property" of the modern poet. The final issue contained his original Latin poem, "Sapphic Verses" (II, 443-444), with a modest note saying, "The verses do not affect poetry; they have no imagination, nor do they pretend even to fancy. Their utmost aim is prettiness . . . their merit, if any, consists entirely in their style and diction." In essence, the poet sends a boy to find flowers worthy of him and his maid, and he ends with a comment on the transience of love and the permanence of goodness.

The article on "Stafford's Niobe" (I, 59-62) is, in a way, a "specimen" essay. Stafford was a contemporary of Shakespeare and his "Niobe" was a 1611 tract that is little more than fulminations against his critics and against women. When Stafford speaks with delight of the effects of the grave upon feminine beauty, Barnes says that it is just as despicable to speak of a beautiful woman as "a mass of putrifying materials" as it is to call her "divine creature" or "goddess", for both extremes are mere cant, "not reason, but raving". Barnes points out two passages which resemble lines in *Paradise Lost* and suggests that Milton may have read them. When Stafford complains of the faults of his age, Barnes recommends the passage to his own contemporaries who complain of the present times and long for the "golden days of our ancestors".

The best of Barnes' essays and one which follows the traditional eighteenth century essay is his "Project for Making Beaux and Belles Useful" in the fourth issue (II, 366-380). While not as shocking as Swift's, his "modest proposal" is more savage than the rest of his essays and shows what he could do as a satirist. Like Lamb in the essay on Burial Societies, he uses the fiction that he has discovered the essay among the effects of a "deceased literary friend". It concerns a species which Linnaeus overlooked, "those barren tracts of moral nature, called Beaux and Belles, which are probably self-produced since they have 'no sexual qualities except mere sex.' " They have power of speech but rarely say anything, they are usually bored, and much of their time is spent in an occupation called ogling. He suggests that the belles be used "as figurantes at the Opera", as mistresses to fashionable young gentlemen in what he calls "Beau-Platonism, being such an intercourse as the philosopher Plato would have recommended if he had been a fashionable rake" (II, 374). The males could join the troops which parade in the park and never fight "except when the citizens happen to be a little refractory at the prospect of starvation or an infringement of their liberties", or they could become pensioners in the House of Commons "to give a vote, when all the eloquence of the Minister had been of no avail" (II, 375, 376). Since the beaux and belles are seldom married, he suggests "engrafting" them with ill-mannered but studious scholars and shrews, with the object of producing sensible people by the third or fourth generation. The essay is related to the *Spectator* essays which relate the dissections of the beau's head and the coquette's heart. It is traditional in form, in its criticism of manners and morals, and in the political satire directed at the corruption of the Perceval administration.

The third issue of thc *Reflector* did not contain the familiar initials "T.B." but evidence exists that Barnes was represented in its pages. "On the Right of Dower out of Personalty" (II, 25-30) concerns property rights of women and is signed "Porcia", and it is patently from the hand and training of a man of law, but only the vagaries of human nature can explain why Barnes did not use his initials. Perhaps his later propensity for anonymity was beginning to make itself evident. Under current laws, married women had no claim to the personalty or personal property of their husbands, and Barnes points out that while society has moved from the primitive to the refined, the law has not kept pace with manners. The article is replete with citations from old and recent laws as well as from Blackstone. Barnes' case is forceful and persuasive, built upon humanitarian grounds, on evidence from his reading, and upon precedents. The strong opening and closing statements give the essay a forceful unity. Like his essay on Propertius, it is persuasive and is written in a direct, first-person style; like his essay on Stafford's Niobe, it reveals Barnes as a strong feminist, an attitude which also came out in some of his theatrical reporting. On the evidence of Barnes' legal training, his persuasive style, and his feminist attitude, only he, of the several principal writers in the *Reflector*, could have written "On the Right of Dower out of Personalty".

Barnes' *Reflector* articles are too limited in scope to enable one to generalize about what he might have done had he devoted his life to *belles lettres* instead of to journalism, as those who knew him well felt able to do. Certainly he did little to further the development of the essay form: his essays are wholly traditional, even imitative. Blunden says that "Barnes was a dramatic critic of deep reading and feeling",[10] but in the *Reflector* he chose to eschew the political and theatrical subjects in which he was engaged daily and on which he no doubt considered Hunt as having a prior claim. Instead, he used the opportunity to indulge his fondness for literary or critical discussion, original Latin poetry, and social satire. Except for a few topical references, it is Barnes the scholar who is writing for the *Reflector*, drawing on his classical background and his current reading and presenting his views in persuasive prose that is a personal communication in its graceful, fluent style. He persuades with facts and reason rather than invective. His journalism experience seems to have prevented his using the inflated rhetoric of many of the older writers, but a lack of depth and insight prevents his essays from becoming memorable literary experiences which transcend the temporal and become universal. He is not a Hazlitt or a Lamb, by any means. In spite of his friends' regret that he was a loss to the literary world, Barnes sought and found his own level with the *Times*, and on that level his achievement was a powerful one.

B. BARRON FIELD

The *Dictionary of National Biography* describes Barron Field as a lawyer and miscellaneous writer, but his name is better re-

[10] Edmund Blunden, *Leigh Hunt's "Examiner" Examined* (New York and London, 1928), p. 36.

membered through footnotes explaining the "B.F." in two of Lamb's essays, "Mackery End, in Hertfordshire" and "Distant Correspondents". Field had a more distinguished name in his ancestry, for Oliver Cromwell was the great-great-grandfather of Field's paternal grandmother. His mother was Esther Barron, and his father, Henry Field (1755-1837), was a prominent London doctor who was elected apothecary to Christ's Hospital in 1807. His older brother, Francis, was a clerk at India House; his younger brother, Frederick (1801-1885), went to Christ's Hospital in 1807 at the age of six as a private pupil of the headmaster. Later Frederick was graduated from Trinity College, Cambridge, and made a name for himself as a specialist in the old church fathers, Origen and Chrysostom.

Barron Field was two years younger than Hunt, having been born on October 23, 1786. He was named Barron after his mother, and his name sometimes gave the impression that he was a nobleman (and misspelled "Baron") and gave his critics the enviable opportunity to call his poetry the harvest from a barren field. Information about his early years is scanty, and no source mentions him as a student at Christ's Hospital. He was only fifteen years old when his name appeared in the subscription list in the first edition of Hunt's *Juvenilia*. He was probably not acquainted with Hunt at the time, for first evidence of their friendship appears in February 1804. In 1805 or 1806 he began writing theatrical reviews for the *Times*, following the example of Hunt's candid reporting in the *News*. From June 20, 1809, to June 23, 1814, he studied law at the Inner Temple and tried to make a living with his pen. He contributed articles to the *Examiner*,[11] the *Reflector*, and the *Quarterly Review*. In 1811 he published a book on Blackstone's *Commentaries* which was highly regarded and frequently reprinted. Field's connection with the *Times* gave his fellow student, Barnes, his start with that paper, and when

[11] For example, his review of *Hamlet* (1808, p. 415) and "Outlines of the History of Covent Garden Theatre" (1808, p. 620). In the preface to the 1809 *Examiner* Hunt expressed his thanks to his critical correspondents, B.F. and H.R. (Henry Robertson, who reviewed operas).

Field resigned as drama critic around 1810, Barnes took over that task.

In 1816 Field married Jane Cairncross, who survived him by many years, living until 1878. They had no children. In 1816 he secured an appointment as advocate-fiscal in Ceylon and later of judge of the supreme court of New South Wales. The germ of Lamb's "Distant Correspondents" is contained in a letter to Field in Australia. He returned to England in 1824, "plump and friendly", in Lamb's words, and practiced law there for the next six years, during which he published several articles on his voyages in the *London Magazine*. In 1830 he went into foreign service again, this time as chief justice at Gibraltar, where Lord Beaconsfield (Disraeli) called on him and later wrote an uncomplimentary characterization of him. Talfourd wrote that he "had a sparkling vivacity".[12] In 1841 Field returned home to Torquay and spent his remaining years editing and publishing plays by Heywood and Legge for the Shakespeare Society. He published a short memoir of Lamb's life in 1836 and wrote a life of Wordsworth which was never published because of the poet's disapproval of it.[13] He wrote some inconsequential poetry, some of it published in the *Examiner*, some in his *First Fruits of Australian Poetry* (1819), reviewed by Lamb in the *Examiner*.[14] He died at Torquay on April 11, 1846.

The original nexus between Barron Field and the Lamb-Hunt group has yet to be satisfactorily established. In the absence of any definite evidence, most biographers have been content with statements which give the impression that Christ's Hospital was the link. But Field did not attend Christ's Hospital and was not even remotely connected with it until 1807, when his father became apothecary and his brother a student there, and by that time Field was twenty and an old employee of the *Times*. Blunden speaks of Barnes, Dyer, and Field as "a set of persons educated in one school",[15] which may have reference to the general

[12] Thomas Noon Talfourd, *Memoirs of Charles Lamb* (Philadelphia, 1892), p. 215.

[13] *Leigh Hunt's "Examiner" Examined*, p. 3.

[14] *Examiner* (January 16, 1820), pp. 39-40. Reprinted in *Works*, I, 197-200.

[15] *Leigh Hunt and His Circle*, p. 61.

school of experience and not Christ's Hospital. Landré says, "A ce premier groupe d'amis de Christ's Hospital il faut ajouter Wood ... James Scholefield ... et le fils du pharmacien de l'école, Barron Field"; in speaking of Lamb's Wednesday gatherings, he mentions, among those present, "Barron Field qu'il connaissait depuis Christ's Hospital."[16] Talfourd's version, that Field "was connected with Lamb by the link of Christ's Hospital associations",[17] is no doubt truthful but misleading since the link is not with Field's associations but with Lamb's. Lucas is more accurate, saying that Field, "though not actually a Christ's Hospitaller, was through his father ... connected with it".[18] Since Field was not a schoolmate of the other *Reflector* contributors, it is possible that he and Lamb were brought together by Field's older brother, Francis, who, like Lamb, was a clerk at East India House, though the eleven years' differences in the ages of Charles and Barron might have proved a hindrance.

Another possibility does not seem to have been suggested or explored, and that is Henry Crabb Robinson as the keystone of the arch between Field and Lamb. Robinson and Field were both working for the *Times* from about 1805 or 1806; Robinson knew Lamb in 1806 (or before) because he was in Lamb's party at the performance of *Mr. H.* on December 10, 1806. Therefore, Field and Lamb may have been acquainted through Robinson in 1806. Field first appears in Robinson's diary under date of January 17, 1812, when Robinson went to Field's late one evening and found Lamb and Hunt there. But since Robinson did not begin his diary until January 1811, this initial citation does not mean that he was not acquainted with Field before that time.

Field's connection with Leigh Hunt was already an old one by 1806, even though the evidence does not indicate what brought the two men together in the first place. Hunt knew Field as early as the winter of 1804, for in a letter to Marianne Kent dated February 23, 1804, Hunt tells her that "Mr. B. F. has been with me this morning and I am happy to say that he was much better

16 Landré, I, 61, 111.
17 *Memoirs of Charles Lamb*, p. 215.
18 *Life*, I, 404.

as to a gentlemanly temperance." [19] At this time Field was a youngster of seventeen; Hunt was a little over nineteen but he had made something of a name for himself with his *Juvenilia.* Neither young man was to begin writing theatrical reviews for another year or so, but some mutual influence propelled them toward the same vocation. The first extant letter from Field to Hunt, dated August 11, 1807, testifies to their continuing friendship and reveals that Hunt also wrote for the *Times*, probably as a substitute during Field's absence on holiday.[20] After Field entered Inner Temple, the two friends joined briefly a group of young law students in a debating society. When Hunt entered Surrey Gaol, he was accompanied by Field, whose efforts made it possible for Hunt to receive visitors at the Gaol. In 1816 Field congratulated Hunt on "the poetical philosophy with which you have found out the soul of goodness in things evil" in *The Story of Rimini*, and soon after Field left for Australia Hunt published Letter VI of his series, "Harry Brown's Letters to his Friends", entitled "To Barron Field". His absence from the country for the next eight years and Hunt's sojourn in Italy from 1822-1825 may have been the causes for the end of what had been a very active friendship.

Field was not only a faithful friend for many years; he was also a faithful contributor to the *Reflector* and, occasionally, to the *Examiner*. In the *Reflector* he published six articles and four short miscellaneous items.

Volume I, Number 1: "Shakespeare Sermons"
"The Law-Student"
"On Early and Late Hours"

Volume I, Number 2: "Is it Justifiable to Reprint the Pruriencies of Our Old Poets?"
"The Law-Student"
Miscellaneous: "What Constitutes a Madman"
"Effects of Wealth"

[19] Brewer, p. 22.
[20] *Leigh Hunt and His Circle*, p. 99.

Volume II, Number 3: "The Law-Student"

Volume II, Number 4: Miscellaneous: "To the Editor of the Reflector"
"Character of an Exaggerator"

Field's articles show a diminution in quantity, starting off with three articles (21 pages) in the first issue, two articles and two notes (16 pages) in the second, one article (9 pages) in the third, and two short notes (5 pages) in the fourth. They are signed with three daggers, and the six major articles are credited to "B. Field" in the British Museum copy. They conform to what one would expect of a lively young law student who is also interested in the Elizabethan drama. Their epistolary nature permits a looseness of organization and an informal tone which lends a modicum of brightness and pleasantry to pages which are rather crowded with the serious.

The three letters entitled "The Law Student" constitute an essay serial in letter form. That the series was to continue is evident from a note in the second that future articles would be concerned with the justice of English laws. The first letter is dated from "Inner Temple, March 27, 1810"; the second and third are dated in April and August of 1811 respectively. These dates destroy the little fiction of the opening letter of transmittal which says, "I enclose you a series of letters" (I, 43) since this would necessitate dating all letters prior to publication of the first *Reflector*. Besides, topical references throughout show that they were composed at about the times they are dated. The first letter (I, 43-52) explains the common law societies of London with something of their history and *modus operandi*. Some of the four Inns of Court and ten Inns of Chancery date back to the days of the Magna Charta and were commissioned to confer degrees. He explains the mechanics of obtaining entrance to the Inns as well as their social and legal customs. Field makes frequent reference to Blackstone, on whose *Commentaries* he published his *Analysis* in the spring of 1811.

The second and third letters are of greater topical interest because they concern contemporary men of the English bar, the attorneys, justices, and serjeants at law who were so prominent not only in the news of the first two decades of the nineteenth century but who entered the lives of Hunt, Byron, and Shelley in more direct ways. The second article (I, 374-380) begins with high praise for Lord Thomas Erskine, the Whig lawyer who withdrew from public life after the beginning of the Regency and to whom "the liberty of the press is indebted", who "never shrank from the defence of an alledged libeller for *reasons of state*" (I, 375). The attorney general, Sir Vicary Gibbs, comes in for a long discussion. He was popular in the 1790's as the defender of Hardy for treason, but after becoming attorney general in 1807 he prosecuted with such diligence that he became very unpopular. Field's picture of Gibbs agrees with that of Hunt in the *Autobiography* and is of particular interest because Gibbs pursued the matter of libel so industriously during the early days of the century. Early in 1813 he stepped down as attorney general and the Hunts were prosecuted by Sir William Garrow, who is described next as he appeared to Field in 1811 as rather less of a gentleman than Sir Vicary, often rude and bullying, with "a talent for intimidating and confounding false-witnesses". Field concludes that, while he would like to succeed in his profession, he "would not have Mr. Garrow's talents for the world" (I, 377-378). The balance of the second article has short characterizations of other barristers: Mr. Park, who is "eloquent only in tears"; Mr. Topping, who is "eloquent only in anger" (I, 379); Mr. Clarke, who prosecuted Drakard for the libel in the *Stamford News*; and Mr. Brougham, who "has very recently brought himself into great and deserved estimation, by his judicious and eloquent defence of Messrs. Hunt, and by his still more elaborate and beautiful one of Mr. Drakard, from a similar charge" (I, 380). Brougham, of course, was the close friend and personal lawyer of Hunt who defended him unsuccessfully in the libel trial in 1812.

The third letter (II, 113-122) is a miscellany of additional uncomplimentary remarks on Gibbs and Garrow, and on those lesser figures of the legal profession, the serjeants at law, a few of whom are still of interest today. Serjeant Shepherd defended Sir Francis Burdett and the "Old Price" cause. Serjeant William Mackworth Praed, father of the poet, is mentioned, as well as Serjeant Rough, later Sir William Rough, lawyer, poet, dramatist, friend of Crabb Robinson, and finally a chief justice in Ceylon. While some of the people mentioned never made their way into biographical dictionaries, many of them were connected with more important people, and Field's first-hand impressions provide us with aspects which we would not otherwise have.

"Shakespeare Sermons" (I, 29-35) in the first issue is supposedly written by a friend of the writer's, a man to whom Shakespeare's works are literally his Bible. Like the Bible, Shakespeare has a concordance and many commentators. All that is lacking are sermons. Field's friend has supplied that deficiency with a sermon based on *Much Ado About Nothing* IV, 2: "But, masters, remember that I am an ass; though it be not written down, yet forget not that I am an ass." It burlesques Methodist preachers "who connect passages of Scripture which have no relevancy, wire-draw their texts till they have no meaning at all, and find out meanings in them which they never meant" (I, 30). Hunt placed this amusing sermon next to another anti-Methodist paper, "On the Pernicious Effects of Methodism in Our Colonies". Another Field article in the first issue, "On Early and Late Hours" (I, 107-115) is a compilation of quotations from his reading and from that of his friend, Mr. Gilchrist, giving the hours of rising, eating, and retiring at various periods of English history beginning with William the Conqueror. Field concludes that the changes have resulted from a postponement of the retirement hour and the increase in the number of evening entertainments. He adds a political side-effect in "the additional facility which these unnatural hours give to the corrupters of Parliament. . . . Thus it is that bad private habits are sure to produce a corresponding viciousness in public ones." He closes with a good punch line: The situation cannot be remedied, "and I myself am now writing against late hours by a midnight lamp" (I, 123).

The last of the full-length articles (I, 365-370) is a dialogue discussing the question, "Is It Justifiable to Reprint the Pruriencies of Our Old Poets?", a discussion which grew out of the recent appearance of Chalmers' 21-volume edition of the English poets, some of whom were expurgated. The first speaker does not approve of expurgation on the grounds that the result is not true to the author and that "the pruriencies of Shakespeare and Dryden *will* go down to posterity along with the rest of their works" (I, 368); even a moralist like Gifford did not delete any passages from his edition of Massinger's plays. A reader "who aspires to an accurate idea of the poets of her country, must go to the fountainheads of them all, however tinctured with impurities may be some of their streams" (I, 369). The second speaker defends Chalmers and quotes an *Examiner* article on pruriency, and he recommends such books as the *Family Shakespeare, Elegant Extracts,* and Lamb's *Specimens of the Old Dramatic Poets*. This is the only "Letter to the Editor" in the *Reflector* which elicited a reply from Hunt, who said that expurgation would have little effect upon the works of the great poets.

The short pieces by Field are interesting for their allusions and for their good-natured fun. "What Constitutes a Madman" (I, 479-482) takes for its basis a Roman law under which a man was declared insane if he was guilty of profusion and waste. Field furnishes a model affidavit which illustrates how easy it is to have someone declared a lunatic and alludes to Hell-Fire Dick, the coachman who drove the route from London to Cambridge and who was very well known in his day.[21] The affidavit names a former student at Cambridge who "used to spend all his time with the drivers of that town", whom he so accurately imitated in all their vulgar habits. "The Effects of Wealth" (I, 482-484) is a two-page whimsy on the *nouveau riche* and those who are out to seek their fortunes. The two little notes in the final issue are both somewhat in the nature of character sketches but quite unlike the Theophrastian character. The first is ostensibly from

[21] Hell-Fire Dick is mentioned by Mary Lamb in a letter to Miss Hutchinson, August 20, 1815 (*Letters*, II, 173). His name was Richard Vaughan, according to E. V. Lucas, *At the Shrine of St. Charles* (London, 1934), pp. 80-81.

the devil, complaining about the too-free use of his name in epithets; the second, "Character of an Exaggerator", contains anecdotes about a man who could not repeat a story without embellishing it beyond all recognition.

Barron Field contributed nothing to the development of the familiar essay or to the corpus of good literature, though his articles are interesting records of some of the people and ideas of his period. For him, writing was a sideline and his essays are primarily informative, following tradition in using a pseudo-epistolary method and in emphasizing manners. "The Law Student" is an essay serial, one entry of which is a dialogue. Field's *Reflector* essays have not been reprinted or anthologized, for they have little of value as literature. Some of them, by their whimsical nature, reveal this man of law and dabbler in the fine arts as the "plump and friendly" member of the Lamb circle and exhibit some of the "sparkling vivacity" which Talfourd found in him. More important, they record verbal pictures of people who were part of the fabric of London life during 1810-1812 and help to fill in some of the spaces surrounding the more important people with whom they rubbed elbows, shared thoughts, meals, and lodgings. In short, they help to re-animate some of the figures of a rather remote past.

C. THOMAS MITCHELL

Though Thomas Mitchell was well known in the first half of the nineteenth century as a translator of Aristophanes, he is remembered now for his association with Leigh Hunt's *Reflector*. He was born in London on May 30, 1783, the son of Alexander Mitchell, a riding master of Grosvenor Place. He was a year and a half older than Hunt, an "Old Blue" who came to Christ's Hospital in June 1790, so he was already well along in school when Hunt arrived in November 1791. His years at Christ's Hospital coincide with those of Hunt and overlap with those of Coleridge, Barnes, Field, and Scholefield; Lamb had left six months before Mitchell arrived. This riding master's son was admitted to Christ's Hospital on presentation of Martyn Fonnereau, Esquire, who later subscribed to Hunt's *Juvenilia.* In October 1802 Mitchell went to Pembroke College, Cambridge, where he was graduated B.A. in 1806 and M.A. in 1809. After holding a fellowship at Sidney Sussex College for two years, he withdrew, not because he objected to the doctrines of the established church, but because he feared the responsibilities of pastoral work.

In the decade after 1806 Mitchell was tutor in three distinguished families. His first charge was a son of Sir George Henry Rose, the diplomat;[22] another was Vernon Smith (1800-1873), who was to have a distinguished political career under Grey, Melbourne, and Russell; around 1816 Mitchell went to the family of Thomas Hope, the wealthy art patron (also a subscriber to Hunt's *Juvenilia*). In 1810 he met William Gifford, beginning a connection which eventually made him a reviewer for the *Quarterly*. His series of articles on Aristophanes was so successful that he later published the translations which established his reputation. He spent the last twenty years of his life in translating and editing, and he was often in straitened circumstances until the government granted him £150 from the royal bounty. He did not marry. He died of apoplexy at his home at Steeple Aston, near Woodstock, on May 4, 1845.

Mitchell is not mentioned in Crabb Robinson's diary, nor does he seem to have been a part of the Lamb circle, though he and Lamb were acquainted. They must have met during visits to Hunt in Surrey Gaol, since Mitchell was there occasionally and the Lambs frequently. Hunt's earliest memory of Mitchell was as a school boy who had achieved a certain eminence as a monitor.

> He was little in person, little in face, and he had a singularly juvenile cast of features, even for one so petit. . . . He had really attained his position prematurely. I rose afterwards to be next to him in the school; and from a grudge that existed between us, owing probably to a reserve, which I thought pride, on his part, and to an ardency which he may be have considered frivolous on mine, we became friends. Circumstances parted us in after-life; I became a Reformist, and he a

22 Another son was William Stewart Rose, the poet and translator mentioned by Hunt in his "Feast of the Poets" (II, 323).

Quarterly Reviewer; but he sent me kindly remembrances not long before he died.[23]

Hunt's friendship with Mitchell continued unabated from their school days until at least 1816, at which time Mitchell was becoming more closely associated with the *Quarterly Review*. Hunt thought highly of Mitchell as a friend and as a writer, even considering the possibility of having Mitchell and Barnes take over the editorship of the *Examiner* during his imprisonment, but whether he discussed the matter with them is not known. Mitchell was a dinner guest at the Gaol in June 1813 along with Byron, Barnes, Moore, Brougham, and Dr. Gooch, and Hunt dedicated his 1814 edition of *The Feast of the Poets* to him. Their close friendship did not prevent Mitchell from reproaching Hunt for giving his opinions "ex cathedra Examinentis", and his tact, candor, and critical perception are displayed in a letter written to Hunt when *The Story of Rimini* appeared in 1816:

> With my eyes yet in tears, I wish to thank you for your Poem. You know my idolatry for Lord Byron, who touches me more than any man except Shakespeare; nothing of his, in my opinion, ever showed more power than *Rimini*. There are passages however which wanted a friend's eye, before they went into the world. You belong to posterity or I would not talk to you thus. Pray let me talk to you sincerely upon this small point.[24]

Although he must have been busy with his tutorial work, Mitchell found time to contribute six small items to his friend's new quarterly magazine in 1811 and 1812. Apparently he wrote nothing for the first two issues; in the third he is represented by three short "Miscellaneous Pieces" and in the fourth by two full articles and one short piece, all signed "M." Hunt did not indicate Mitchell's authorship for any articles in the British Museum copy of the *Reflector*.

Volume II, Number 3: Miscellaneous: "Inquiries Respecting Jack Ketch, and the Oldest Man Alive"

[23] *Autobiography*, p. 104.
[24] Brewer, pp. 87-88.

"Lines on Hearing Certain Protestations Made by Sir C– P– M.D."
"A Pair of Portraits"

Volume II, Number 4: "Classical Antiquity of the English Language"
"Reflexions on the Letters of Mademoiselle l'Espinasse. Written between the years 1773 and 1776, inclusive. Published at Paris 1809"
Miscellaneous: "On the Eddystone Lighthouse"

Mitchell's "Reflexions on the Letters of Mademoiselle l'Espinasse" (II, 334-342) is a commentary rather than a critical review of the book which had been published a year or two before. L'Espinasse was originally a companion to the Marchioness du Deffand, famous as a hostess to many prominent men of France in the middle of the eighteenth century; later she formed her own coterie, which included the Comte de Guibert, to whom these letters are addressed. Mitchell is mainly interested in communicating his impression of the foolish lengths to which this woman permitted her passion – and her pen – to go. His comments reflect the ideas of Voltaire, Rousseau, and the Romantics: "The virtues, which she valued in herself and which she expected in others were an entire abandonment to the feelings, a ready acquiescence in first emotions, an approximation to a state of nature, and to the simplicity and sincerity of savage life . . . agitation, suffering, and feeling were the food on which her mind subsisted" (II, 339). Mitchell comments that some people have had adventures which surpass any romance, and he concludes, somewhat like Puck: "Truly the whole world are fools, and the wise are more so than the rest" (II, 342).

The second full-length essay by Mitchell is a delightful spoof entitled "Classical Antiquity of the English Language" (II, 324-334), built on the reverse premise that ancient Greek has derived many expressions from modern English. Some of his examples require a knowledge of Greek for their appreciation, but others do not: Bellerophon, he says, is a corruption of the English term "Billy Ruffian"; Diomed comes from that warrior's vow of chastity, to "Die a maid"; and Alexander the Great is from Alexander's antipathy for eggs and his instructions to throw "All eggs under the grate" (II, 324). His humor becomes satire when he brings in the politicians, saying that Chatham's disastrous expedition to Walcheren is exemplified in a passage in Herodotus, literally translated as "throwing away many brave men" (II, 327). In a reversal of thesis, he says that the English passion for beef derives from ancient religious rites, and their passion for horses and racing comes from a passage in Amphysciarius stating "that to see a horse at full speed was a sort of mystery". This topic permits Mitchell to conclude with a digression on coachmanship derived from his acquaintance with Tilliamant Bobart, the driver of the Oxford coach, known to most of the Hunt circle, and a character in Hunt's *Indicator* essay, "Coaches" (1820).

Mitchell's first contribution to the *Reflector* is a letter (II, 203-206) to Mr. Reflector inspired by his having read Lamb's essay, "On the Inconveniences of Being Hanged" in the second issue. His curiosity has been aroused by Jack Ketch and his letter consists of two pages of amusing speculations about the race of Ketches, or Ketchidae. He hopes that Pensilis, who "knows what it is to be in a state of suspence", will relieve his curiosity about the genus Ketch. To the letter is added a postscript which ostensibly concerns an unidentified "oldest man alive" but which is really a short political satire, full of allusions to recent events. Another two-part letter from Mitchell is "A Pair of Portraits" (II, 212-215), two short character sketches describing the landlord of an inn and an elderly retired woman from whom he rented rooms in New Forest. Again Mitchell's sense of humor predominates, expressed in the small details which make a "character" come alive on the page. The two remaining "Short Miscellaneous Pieces" are in verse. One is a parody on Horace's ode, "Carmina", and is entitled "Lines on Hearing Certain Protestations Made by Sir C– P– M.D." (II, 208), with allusions which are now obscure. The other is a letter

(II, 440-443) containing two poems, one an original Latin poem on "wreckling" or "spearing eels" and the other, which he says was written by a former law professor at Oxford, Dr. Joseph Phillimore, in praise of Eddystone Lighthouse.

While Mitchell's later writings carried him into the more erudite field of classical criticism and translation, his essays for the *Reflector* exhibit a sense of humor, a tongue-in-cheek quality, and observation and appreciation of individuals as characters. One feels that he and Lamb would have enjoyed each other since the same qualities are so prominent in Lamb's personal essays; had circumstances not channeled his energies in a different direction, he might have made a more lasting fame as a companion to Elia than as the translator of Aristophanes. One can easily understand why Hunt, with his strong propensity for friendship, found one of his closest friends in this scholarly and sociable young man of about his own age. His style – light, satirical, pointed, unpedantic – is suited to his material, and his comments provide a bright spot in the *Reflector*.

D. JAMES SCHOLEFIELD

In the second quarter of the nineteenth century James Scholefield was a well-known classical scholar and professor of Greek, but today he is remembered as a friend of Leigh Hunt and contributor to the *Reflector*. He was five years younger than Hunt and another of the several Bluecoat boys who were to remain his good friends for so many years. The exact date of his arrival at Christ's Hospital is not known, but he would have been about eight years old, placing it approximately 1797 and giving him and Hunt a year or two together at school. In his *Autobiography* Hunt mentions Scholefield twice: as a fellow student who later "attained an extraordinary succession of university honours" and as a contributor to the *Reflector*.[25] Scholefield was still alive when the *Autobiography* came out in 1850, but the two men had not corresponded for many years. But when Hunt was working on

[25] *Autobiography*, pp. 56, 214.

James Scholefield, 1789-1853

(Engraving by J. B. Hunt)
(Copyright, National Portrait Gallery)

Lord Byron and Some of His Contemporaries (published in January 1828), Scholefield's recent appointment as Regius Professor of Greek at Cambridge was fresh in his memory. What he had to say about Scholefield was not included in that volume – it was among the rejected pages of manuscript now in the Brewer Collection of the University of Iowa – but those pages show that Hunt's impression of Scholefield as a boy was still vivid thirty years later:

> Scholefield . . . I remember seeing for the first time, when he was a stout little boy, standing on the Grammar School steps, very neat & self-possessed, with a sanguine complexion, & not without an air of superiority. The recollection is particularly strong upon me, because I set him down for a future scholar, & wondered that I had never seen him before. This is now the successor of Porson. I have not seen him for many years. His opinions, no doubt, on many things are different from mine; but he could hardly have seen his new title in the papers, with greater pleasure than I did.[26]

Scholefield was born on November 15, 1789, at Henley-on-Thames, the son of an independent minister; his life of devotion to Greek scholarship ended on August 4, 1853, at Hastings, where he is buried. After his death, his wife published a memoir of his life. They had one son, Rev. J. E. Scholefield of Warwick. After distinguishing himself at Christ's Hospital, Scholefield entered Trinity College, Cambridge, in 1809, just a little under twenty years of age. The great Richard Porson had been dead a year and Peter Paul Dobree (whose works Scholefield was to edit in the 1830's) was the Regius Professor of Greek. Scholefield advanced steadily. In 1812 he was elected to the Craven University Scholarship; the next year he was ordained, and in 1816 he took his M.A. In 1823 he was appointed to the curacy of St. Michael's, Cambridge, a position he held until his death, and that year saw the publication of the first of his many books. His highest honor came in 1826 with his appointment as the successor of Porson and Dobree. He was a successful teacher and writer, a good examiner and speaker. Besides editing the works of Dobree (1831-1835) and of Bishop Pilkington (1842), he edited Porson's *Four Tragedies of Euripides* (1828) and put out an edition of

[26] *Leigh Hunt's Autobiography, The Earliest Sketches*, pp. 33-34.

Aeschylus in 1828 and his *Parallel Greek and English Testament* in 1836.

As the youngest of the Christ's Hospital alumni who wrote for the *Reflector*, Scholefield was not a part of the Hunt or Lamb circles in London. He is not mentioned by Lamb or Robinson, nor did Hunt leave documentary evidence as to how he happened to write for the *Reflector*. Hunt may have kept in touch with the young scholar in the decade or so after leaving school and then suggested that he contribute to the new magazine. After putting out the first issue of the *Reflector*, Hunt went to Cambridge and spent a few days with Scholefield, from January 4 to 8, 1811. Since both had been senior Deputy Grecians, they had much in common. Like Lamb, Hunt had missed out on admission to the university because he stuttered, but he felt close to the scholarly life. The two men corresponded on literary matters during 1811 and 1812, but after this the connection was broken off, for Hunt was soon to go to prison and Scholefield was busy working toward his M.A.

Scholefield's *Reflector* articles were his first published works. Evidence of Scholefield in the magazine must be based upon Hunt's statement that Scholefield wrote for the magazine, upon the signature "S" appended to certain essays, and upon the fact that these certain essays could logically come from Scholefield's pen. But Hunt neglected to identify the Scholefield writings in the British Museum copy of the magazine; as for the "S" signature, the habit of anonymity in practice at the time frequently resulted in cryptic signatures which had no logical connection with the authors. In fact, two of the essays signed "S" could not have been written by Scholefield and must remain anonymous, but they will be examined in relation to Scholefield's contributions. In the first issue Scholefield's articles bear pseudonyms, "Philo-Tragicus" and "Vindex", and five of the seven articles signed "S" can be attributed to him without hesitation.

Volume I, Number 1: "Greek and English Tragedy" (Signed "Philo-Tragicus")
"Dr. Bentley" (Signed "Vindex")

Volume I, Number 2: "Greek and English Tragedy" (Signed "S")
"Poets at College" (Signed "S")

Volume II, Number 3: "Greek and English Tragedy" (Signed "S")

Volume II, Number 4: "Defects in Classical Education" (Signed "S")
"Professor Porson Vindicated" (Signed "S")

Although Scholefield's first *Reflector* article is signed "Philo-Tragicus" rather than his initial, it is obviously the first part of an essay serial and the essays are further linked by a common purpose and style. The first of the series on "Greek and English Tragedy" (I, 62-72) is a general comparison of the excellencies of Greek and English tragedy, opposing Aeschylus to Shakespeare, Sophocles to Rowe, and Euripides to Otway; the second and third have subtitles indicating their special emphasis and contain a number of quotations from the six poets.

The similarities which Scholefield finds in the three pairs of poets makes his task an easy one. Both Aeschylus and Shakespeare lived in times which were favorable for the display of their genius. The drama was uninhibited by restrictions, stage customs were somewhat barbaric, and both Greece and England were fortunate to have great poets at those times. Their "distinguishing characteristic is a daring sublimity of genius" (I, 63). Both dealt with terror, as in *Prometheus* and *Macbeth*, and both used the pathetic incidentally. Both made frequent use of compound epithets. But Shakespeare's flights were higher and he "continues longer on the wing" than Aeschylus. "To Shakespeare, then, all Greece must yield the victory" (I, 66), and this is the theme of the three essays.

In comparing Sophocles and Rowe, Scholefield says that both poets were plagiarists, though Sophocles "borrowed from modesty" and Rowe from "want of genius" (I, 67). Sophocles improved his material and Rowe downgraded it. As to Euripides and Otway, Scholefield says that "the chief excellence is their skill with the pathetic" (I, 69) and he refuses to judge between them. While neither writer is deficient in sublimity, he says that Euripides writes with "the genuine language of true feeling, not only unfabricated, but almost unassisted, by art" (I, 70), a significant comment which reflects the Romantic attitude.

The second in this essay serial (I, 273-283) concerns three illustrious murderesses, Medea, Clytemnestra, and Lady Macbeth, comparing the delineation of their characters, and again Scholefield comments on Euripides' capacity for pathos as parallel to that quality in Otway. Lady Macbeth's character differs from the other two in that her ambition is a challenge to sympathy, and her subtlety in countering the doubts of Macbeth is evidence of Shakespeare's great knowledge of human nature. He considers Lady Macbeth's dismissal of her guests as one of the most sublime scenes "that ever poet imagined", and the final scene is "a strong and frightful example of the folly, the danger, and the wickedness of ambition" (I, 281, 282).

The final article in the series (II, 127-139) compares *Oedipus* and *King Lear*. Since the unities of time and place restricted the Greek poets to "the narrow limits of twenty-four hours of natural time, and somewhat more than the same number of square feet of deal boards", their works do not contain the "astonishing variety of incident and passion" which Shakespeare crowds into his plays (II, 127). Combining the two Oedipus plays into a unit makes them comparable to *King Lear*, although Scholefield points out that the catastrophe (expulsion) in the Oedipus story is not as natural as that in Lear because it is brought about by the oracle rather than Oedipus' own acts. This accentuates an "essential difference between the Greek and English tragedy: the one is a picture of art, the other of nature" (II, 131). In spite of Shakespeare's punning, profanity, and occasional indecencies, his excellences are many, and Scholefield again emphasizes Romantic attitudes in commending Shakespeare as "a master of feeling", a quality which lifts him "above the head of Sophocles, in the delineation of any character of complicated passion", for the imagination is "the great test of genius" (II, 132, 133). *King*

Lear was still being performed in England in Nahum Tate's revision, and Scholefield says that Tate, "having unfortunately more influence in the theatre than taste and the memory of Shakespeare, altered entirely Shakespeare's beautiful original, burlesqued its pathos, destroyed its simplicity, and degraded its every excellence . . . and this drama of Tate's is actually in existence to this day as one of the acting plays of our Theatres Royal!" Then he adds a line reminiscent of Hunt's attitude, that in any discussion of taste, "theatre managers are of course excluded" (II, 138).

"Poets at College" (I, 435-439) is a five-page commentary on Walter Scott's *Life of Dryden* (1808). Since Scholefield is so uncomplimentary about it, and since Hunt was also critical of Scott in the *Reflector*,[27] one wonders if the two men may have discussed Scott when Hunt visited Scholefield early in the year. Scholefield says, in essence, that information about the college life of poets, and Dryden's in particular, is very limited, that this period of their lives is very important because it covers the formative period of a poet's mind.

The fourth issue of the *Reflector* contained four articles signed "S" but only two of them are by Scholefield. "Defects in Classical Education" (II, 232-235) begins, perhaps coincidentally, as the third "Greek and English Tragedy" ended, with a quotation from Gifford's translation of Juvenal. His theme is simple: the study of the classics is worthwhile, but it should be cleared of many of its encumbrances in order to make it more attractive to young students. The writings of the ancients contain great treasuries of wisdom, but they emphasize unduly such superfluities as a knowledge of genealogy of the gods, their crimes and their adulteries, which may corrupt the students. Again Scholefield concludes with a line which shows his affinity to Hunt: "Taste, after all, is the quality which must arrange, digest, and give life to knowledge" (II, 235).

"Professor Porson Vindicated" (II, 236-243) is an answer to an article by Dr. Samuel Butler, headmaster of Shrewsbury School and later Bishop of Litchfield and Coventry, criticizing Porson

[27] In his footnotes to "The Feast of the Poets", II, 316.

for showing contempt for his literary contemporaries. Scholefield mentions Porson's praise of Dr. Charles Burney and maintains that whatever Porson said of the others was justified. Scholefield speaks of what Butler might do if he were to become the Regius Professor – a distinction which Butler did not attain, but Scholefield himself did. There is little reason to doubt that this article was written by Scholefield, the young classics scholar at Cambridge, where Porson's memory was still fresh.

Likewise Scholefield undoubtedly wrote the article in defense of Bentley in the first issue and signed "Vindex" or Avenger (I, 158-165). Dr. Richard Bentley (1662-1742) was the predecessor of Porson at Trinity College, and Scholefield defends him against Pope's picture of him in the *Dunciad*. Reportedly Bentley said of Pope's translation of Homer, "The verses are good verses, but the work is not Homer, – it is Spondanus" (I, 165) [28] and Pope had his revenge on Bentley by putting him in his satire. Like the article on Porson, this is another vindication and it concerns another Regius Professor at Trinity College – and loyalty to one's college would be sufficient for Scholefield to defend two illustrious men of Trinity. Scholefield was the only Trinity man among Hunt's friends at this time. Both articles call the criticism a libel, and they are similar in structure, starting with quotations and ending persuasively. Both include the line from Book IV of the *Dunciad* in which Bentley is called "Aristarchus" and both contain many quotations. In the one article Scholefield calls Bentley's edition of Milton "A monster whose vices were not redeemed by a single virtue" (a line from a Satire of Juvenal) and in the other he says that Porson's admirers made him out to be a "faultless monster which the world ne'er saw" (a line from a John Sheffield essay).

The seven articles which are attributable to Scholefield with confidence show a unity of style and area of interest. They use quotations in varying degrees; they show an expected familiarity with the classics, with Shakespeare, and with later playwrights;

[28] Hunt agreed with Bentley, as witness his comment on lines from Pope's translation of the *Iliad* in a footnote (I, 16): "As to the passage in Mr. Pope, it is elegant verse, but no translation at all."

and they have a common viewpoint running through them. Internal evidence points to Scholefield: his specialty of the classics and his presence in Trinity College, Cambridge. One of Scholefield's qualities, according to his obituary, was his "logical arrangement of his matter".[29] These expository and persuasive essays are capably organized, never pedantic, always lucid and fluent; their conclusions are expressed in a forceful recapitulation such as one would expect of a budding curate.

Volume II, Number 4: "Athens and England" (Signed "S")
"On the Change of Structure Induced on Animals by Domestication" (Signed "S")

Of the two remaining articles bearing the "S" signature, the considerable doubt that the "S" stands for Scholefield makes one wish that the editor had prevented the confusion by recording the name of the author in the British Museum copy. "Athens and England" (II, 419-428) draws a parallel between conditions reported by Demosthenes in fourth century B.C. Athens and England of 1811, and the author's opening statement in his thesis: "To learn caution from the events of former ages, and to grow wise from the calamitous experience of other nations . . . ought to be the first object and the noblest distinction of a thinking people" (II, 419). The last words of the quotation, "a thinking people", were favorites of Leigh Hunt and appear frequently in the *Reflector* and the *Examiner*. Again echoing a phrase often tossed at the government by Hunt, the writer says that the country is just waiting for something to "turn up" (II, 422). The Athenians, like the English, had mercenary troops, but British troops have a talent for attacking their friends and increasing the number of the enemies. "Perhaps, the German soldiers are necessary to enforce obedience to military flogging" (II, 424), he writes – a topical reference to the recent furor about flogging in the army and over which the *Stamford News* and the *Examiner* were prosecuted for libel. Another topical reference is the mention of pensions and sinecures. The opening quotation from

[29] *Gentleman's Magazine*, XXIX n.s. (June 1853), 664.

Aristophanes concerns libel, and as the writer points out, publishing the painful truth results in its distortion into libel; those who detect the truth are the ones who expose themselves to danger. Therefore, history's lesson, that similar causes produce similar effects, should show that England too could fall to a foreign conqueror; she should guard the liberty of the press and guard against the fate that befell Athens by a renewal of public spirit and virtue and by constitutional reform.

The fact that this essay is liberally sprinkled with Greek quotations is the only one which justifies its attribution to Scholefield, but others in the Hunt coterie were Greek scholars. The essay is well organized, persuasive, and forcefully concluded, qualities typical of Scholefield, but Scholefield was not interested in politics to the extent that he would write so polemical an article. Its style and subject matter are foreign to the rest of Scholefield's *Reflector* essays. Others of the coterie could have written this article. Barnes was a Greek scholar and he was close to the political scene as a parliamentary reporter. Since he was part of the Hunt circle and the group which talked politics at the home of Thomas Hill, their discussions would account for the homogeneity of ideas and expressions, and Barnes could combine the classical learning with the editorial, the journalistic, and the political orientation of the essay. Then, too, since Barnes signed some of his articles in the *Champion* three or four years later with "Strada", an essay signed "S" could be by him also. Thomas Mitchell was a Greek scholar, a specialist in Aristophanes at a later date, and this article begins with a quotation from Aristophanes, but here the similarity ends. The style is unlike the gentle humor of Mitchell's writing, and we have no evidence that Mitchell was concerned with politics. Except that the essay is not in Hunt's literary style, he too could have written it, as he knew Greek and the classics to some extent and his oft-used term, "a thinking people", points in his direction. But Hunt delighted in needling the administration, and if he had written the article, he would have put his name to it. Perhaps Scholefield wrote the article and Hunt used his editoiral prerogative to re-mold it after his own fashion. No firm reason exists for assigning this article to any one of the Hunt coterie; only the "S" makes Scholefield the doubtful primary candidate.

"On the Change of Structure Induced on Animals by Domestication" (II, 380-387) is signed with an "S" but its remote subject matter and its internal factual evidence eliminate Scholefield as its author. The first part of the essay reflects the early gropings toward the theory of evolution, but the writer is careful to circumvent criticism of his views by fundamentalists. The second part concerns adaptation in animals, and one statement is undeniable evidence that James Scholefield did not write the article:

> The author of this paper has been informed by his highly-respected friend, Mr. Mungo Park, whose evidence on every subject is entitled to the most implicit reliance, that the Dogs of the interior of Africa are of a tawny colour, and formed much like the Wolf. (II, 383).

Mungo Park was a famous African explorer who made two long and dangerous expeditions exploring the Niger River. He returned to Scotland briefly in the years 1798 through 1804, but on his second expedition he was given up for dead by 1806. Thus he had been missing and presumed dead for five or six years when this article was published, yet the reference is in the present tense. During the seven years that Park was in Great Britain, Scholefield was a young boy at Christ's Hospital, evidence which would eliminate Scholefield as author of the article, if one were to overlook the fact that the subject is so foreign to Scholefield and his interests. The most likely author, among the known contributors to the *Reflector*, would be Dr. John Aikin, an older man and one with scientific interests and background. Hunt did not indicate the author in the British Museum copy of the *Reflector*.

The "stout little boy" of Christ's Hospital days became famous as a scholar, teacher, and preacher in later life, but his work in the *Reflector* gives the impression of a good student and perceptive commentator rather than a probing researcher. His more scholarly work was to come later. His essays would have appealed to the intellectuals and would have been a means of improving the public taste. For a young man barely out of his teens, Scholefield demonstrated a fair ability to perceive, to analyze, to organize, and to write in clear and logical style. Like many of the younger writers in the *Reflector*, he was somewhat of a beginner as a periodical essayist, and with the benefit of hindsight one can conclude that, while his contributions were worthwhile, they do not generate regrets that his career (and the discontinuance of the *Reflector*) deprived us of further essays from him.

V

OTHER CONTRIBUTORS TO THE *REFLECTOR*

The advent of a new magazine was undoubtedly welcome news to certain professional writers and acquaintances of Leigh Hunt. Dr. John Aikin, George Dyer, and Octavius Gilchrist contributed articles to the *Reflector* under various signatures and pseudonyms; some of the articles are not signed but contain internal evidence which permits their identification. A few articles in the magazine were written by anonymous contributors who unfortunately remain unidentified. Speculation as to their identity must rest upon subject matter and style, on the basis of which two articles can be attributed to Robert Hunt. Aikin, Dyer, and Gilchrist added the weight of their professional reputations – and a considerable number of pages – to the new periodical and, along with the anonymous writers, made a worthwhile contribution to Leigh Hunt's *Reflector*.

A. DR. JOHN AIKIN

The name of John Aikin was a highly respected one in literary circles in the early years of the nineteenth century; today it survives only as an interesting name far out on the periphery of the circle of Romantic period writers, one of the most minor of the minor essayists and editors. Despite his prominence during his lifetime, he is remembered only for his occasional appearances in the lives of other writers. But the venerable doctor was a genuine friend of letters, a perceptive commentator on poetry, and a writer of grace and elegance.

Dr. Aikin was born at Kibworth in 1747 into a distinguished and capable family. His father was for many years the head of Warrington Academy, which numbered Enfield, Priestley, and Wakefield among its tutors. His sister was Anna Letitia Barbauld, known for her *Hymns in Prose for Children,* a quantity of poetry, and the fifty-volume *British Novelists* (1810), which she edited. The doctor's children were all professional people. Arthur was a chemist and writer; Charles was a doctor and son-in-law of Gilbert Wakefield; Edmund was an architect; and Lucy was a writer. Aikin practiced medicine at Yarmouth until his dissenting political and religious views injured his professional prospects, and he spent the rest of his life in or near London, where he found a congenial atmosphere for his increasing literary output and a circle of friends that included many prominent men of the day. His fine intellect declined to imbecility in his last year or two. When Robinson heard of his death in December 1822, he wrote, "He was in his better days a man of talents, and of the highest personal worth, – one of the salt of the earth." [1] In 1823 Lucy Aikin published her *Memoir of John Aikin, M.D.*, in which she reprinted a number of her father's essays, two of them from the *Reflector*.

The list of Dr. Aikin's publications is an imposing one, numbering nearly fifty in the years from 1770 to 1816. The subjects reflect the broad scope of his interests and his intellect, ranging from papers on gangrene and hemorrhages to poetry and the classics. His *Kalendar of Nature* (1784), a study of the plants and animals around Southampton, was used by Hunt in writing his description of the successive beauties of the year, *The Months* (1821).[2] Dr. Aikin, his sister, and his daughter all contributed to son Arthur's *Annual Review,* published between 1803 and 1808, and Aikin himself edited *The Athenaeum,* a hundred-page monthly magazine of miscellaneous articles, from 1807 to 1809. Towards the end of 1812 Dr. Aikin became editor of Dodsley's *Annual Register*.

1 *Diary*, I, 480.
2 Landré, II, 386.

Dr. John Aitken

(Painting by J. Donaldson, engraving by C. Knight)
(Copyright, National Portrait Gallery)

Among his friends Dr. Aikin could include Priestley, Darwin, Robert Southey, and Gilbert Wakefield, as well as John Howard, the philanthropist, whose literary executor and biographer he was. He was probably acquainted with Hannah Moore, Maria Edgeworth, Samuel Rogers, and Wordsworth, who were friends of Mrs. Barbauld, since she lived with him after 1802. Henry Crabb Robinson first mentions him in March 1801 when he dined at the doctor's; he called on the Aikins on April 12, 1812, and the conversation abounded with praise of Lamb: "The doctor termed him a brilliant writer."[3] What is apparently the only recorded meeting of Aikin and Lamb occurred on May 28, 1814, when Robinson and the two Lambs spent the evening at the Aikin home, but other casual contacts may have occurred. Likewise no recorded evidence of the first acquaintance of Aikin with Leigh Hunt has turned up, but they certainly knew a great deal about each other whether they had social relations or not. Dr. Aikin subscribed to Hunt's *Juvenilia* (1801) and was on the same side of the political and religious fences as Hunt, and Hunt would have known the Aikin family by their writings. Hunt's first mention of Aikin occurs in a letter of December 1810 when he was putting together the first issue of the *Reflector*. Years later, in his *Autobiography*, Hunt makes only a passing reference to the doctor as a contributor to the *Reflector*, but in 1812 he looked upon Aikin's contributions with considerably more respect.

Dr. Aikin contributed a total of eleven items, 134 pages, to the *Reflector*. Four of his articles are anonymous, but the remainder are signed with his initials; his authorship was acknowledged by Hunt in the British Museum copy of the *Reflector*, where Hunt spelled the name "Aitkin". The doctor writes with an easy, natural sentence structure, avoiding involutions, digressions, or inflated rhetoric. Two of the articles are in letter form, addressed to the editor or an imaginary person: one is a personal essay, and the others are expository essays or compilations with an occasional personal opinion.

[3] *Diary*, I, 243.

Volume I, Number 1: "On the Modes of Living and Thinking about the Middle of Last Century" (Signed "JA")
"On War" (Signed "JA")

Volume I, Number 2: "Inquiries Concerning Instinct: Exhibiting a Brief View of the Mental Faculties of the Lower Animals Compared with Those of Man; and Also the State of Opinions on This Subject. Essay I." (Signed "Philosophicus")

Volume II, Number 3: "A Comparison between Thomson and Cowper as Descriptive Poets" (Signed "JA")
"A General Outline of the Philosophy of Sense and Perception. Part I." (Signed "Philosophicus")
Miscellaneous: "On the Word Humour" (Signed "JA")
"Optimism" (Signed "JA")

Volume II, Number 4: "On the Privileges of a Pedestrian" (Signed "A Peripatetic")
"Letters on Biography. Letter I" (Signed "JA")
"On the Origin, Progress, Corruptions, and Gradual Improvement of Medical Science" (Unsigned)
Miscellaneous: "On Assessments" (Signed "JA")

Aikin's article "On the Modes of Living and Thinking about the Middle of Last Century" (I, 114-125) is an assembly of interesting facts which the doctor gleaned from his reading of essay periodicals of the 1750's. He has been reading four of them, but for his present purpose he rejects the *Rambler* of Dr. Johnson, whose essays "betray the very limited knowledge of the world to which the author's situation confined him", and the *Adventurer* of John Hawkesworth, "who surveyed society at a distance, rather than mingled with it" (I, 115). Aikin selected material from the *World*, edited by Edward Moore, whose papers abound "with draughts of the reigning follies and foibles drawn from actual observation", and from the *Connoisseur*, written by George Colman the Elder and Bonnell Thornton, because it was vivacious, pert, light, and superficial, "good authority for the manners and opinions that then floated upon the surface of common society" (I, 115). Hunt too knew and loved the *Connoisseur* essays and acknowledged their influence: "their lively papers . . . gave me an entirely fresh and delightful sense of the merits of essay-writing".[4]

From the two periodicals Dr. Aikin extracted various facts which may have held a special charm for him in memories of his boyhood. He comments about styles of dress, taste in building, furniture, food, drink, gambling, and amusements. In religion and morals some writers were advocating free thinking and seemed to be contemptuous of order and decency, to which Aikin comments, "If the superior classes are not become more moral, they are at least better observers of decorum – which indeed, is a species of morality" (I, 123). Romances and novels of the day were frequently indecent, whereas in his own day, "if modern novels do not often merit an elevated place in the literary scale, they rarely offend against morals or decorum" (I, 124) – this written in the days of Monk Lewis and Mrs. Radcliffe and before Scott and Austen.

Dr. Aikin's second article is "On War" (I, 147-158) and is no doubt the article which Hunt mentions in a letter to Marianne, dated a Saturday evening in December 1810, as helping to delay the debut of the *Reflector*:

After all, the Reflector will not be out till next week, for my articles were not in time to allow the stitching of the sheets, and Dr. Aikin who furnishes another is not ready with it.[5]

[4] *Autobiography*, p. 139.

[5] Brewer, p. 51.

This expository article begins with the familiar question as to whether war is caused by the nature of man or by an imperfect government. England's geographical isolation should be conducive to security and peace, but she has been almost constantly at war because of "an ambitious king, the intrigues of a rash minister, or the machinations of those who have so often succeeded in kindling the flames of war for their own interests" (I, 157-158). His panacea is the same as Hunt's: an independent parliament that reflects the general will of the people.

Aikin's essay on Thomson and Cowper as descriptive poets (II, 43-52) is his best essay in the *Reflector*, and it may have been written as a by-product of the re-issue of his edition of *The Seasons* in 1811. It is one of the essays collected and reprinted in Lucy Aikin's *Memoir,* though the *Reflector* is not mentioned in that volume. Its greatest interest today and probably its greatest value in 1811 is its approving statement of so many of the principles of the preface to the *Lyrical Ballads*, though Wordsworth is not mentioned. Aikin compares the poets' way of describing natural objects in *The Seasons* (1728) and *The Task* (1785), good choices for illustrating the pre-Romantic tendencies of the eighteenth century. His requirements for descriptive poetry seem to echo Wordsworth's:

> To select a variety of circumstances which shall identify the object, and at the same time present it to the imagination in strong and lively colouring, is the essence of poetical description . . . . Grand and sublime objects are best described by a few bold touches; for greatness is lost by being parcelled into minute portions; but objects of beauty and curiosity will bear to be viewed microscopically. (II, 43-44).

Aikin points out that Thomson uses "a mixture of high-wrought language with a humble topic" (II, 44) and humanizes all animals, resulting in action "minutely told in a tragical style that would suit the murder of a Duncan or a Clarence"; he uses compound epithets "with no regard to grammatical propriety"; and he becomes turgid when he elevates "a humble topic by a pomp of phrase" (II, 46-47). Cowper, on the other hand, uses a style that is "purely English, not disdaining a mixture of common words, and rendered poetical . . . by expressions warmed with the vivid imagery that played before his fancy"; he writes with "masculine vigour of vernacular diction" (II, 47-48). Cowper pries "more closely into surrounding scenes" and "his observations are commonly of a more curious and recondite kind" (II, 49). Thomson's personifications are obvious pieces of mechanism, while Cowper's are a result of his "powerful imagination. . . . His personified figures of Winter and of Evening . . . clearly establish his claim to a higher seat on Parnassus than that occupied by Thomson" (II, 50). Thomson is "little suited to the narrative of common life" and his language is wholly unlike that of real conversation, but Cowper understood and used common speech and his story of Crazy Kate and the episodes from his own life illustrate his skill in natural narrating. Thus Aikin agrees with Wordsworth in his emphasis on the imagination and fancy, on common or rural life, on the close view of nature, on a natural and unaffected manner, and on a minimum of personification. "Nothing denotes the mind of a poet so much as this operation of the fancy when objects are presented to the external senses" (II, 49).

Three of the items bearing Dr. Aikin's initials are of little importance: two word studies (II, 197-200) and some information on assessments (II, 449) which he submits as evidence of a need for reapportionment. The fourth is entitled "Letters on Biography" (II, 243-249) and is the first of an unfinished series. It appeared in the final issue of the *Reflector* and, shorn of its epistolary guise, in the *Memoir* under the title "On Self-Biographers". In it he advises a young friend that he include biography in his reading because it helps in predicting human actions, though autobiographies must be read with skepticism because they are written with a view to showing their subject to the world in a favorable light.

Dr. Aikin's four anonymous articles in the *Reflector* continue the use of reason, logic, and good organization exhibited in his signed articles. He was an assiduous compiler of information which emerged in his "survey" articles, serving his readers by investigating what had been done in certain areas and binding this information together with perceptive observations which show that he was no superficial explorer. That his productivity and ambition were without limits is attested by his beginning four essay serials in the *Reflector*. As a man of science he was not one to accept the word of an authority without question, for his own observations support his disagreement with the older writers; he retained scientific objectivity and independence of thought, though he had an unscientific tendency to attribute to God all the things that cannot otherwise be explained. Few writers on scientific subjects would quote poetry as evidence, but Aikin quotes a Cowper poem in a scientific essay. The two articles signed "Philosophicus" and the one on medical science continue Aikin's characteristics of writing essay serials, of writing surveys, and of making astute comments on the writings of his predecessors; the fourth is a personal essay.

The essay on instinct (I, 297-332) concludes that, since animals have both instinct and reason, man's principal advantage is his power of language. Aikin's purpose in writing is to bring "mental philosophy" or the "science of mind" into fashion. He does not use *psychology*, which dates from 1785, but an older word, *pneumatology*. Actions are divided into rational, habitual, mechanical, and instinctive, and instinct is defined as a tendency to do spontaneously certain actions necessary for the preservation and continuation of the kind. Descartes' belief that lower animals are mere machines is contradicted by Aikin on the basis of Locke's findings and his own observations, which revealed that some animals have reasoning power.

Dr. Aikin traces ideas on sensation and perception (II, 77-113) as far back as two thousand years. Sensation is defined as the change produced in the state of the mind by an impression made on a sense organ, of which the sense of touch is the first exercised. Perception is the knowledge of the existence of matter and its qualities and is an active quality producing agreeable or disagreeable feelings in the mind and the wish for its continuance or discontinuance. Locke, Reid, and Stewart are quoted and in some cases refuted, and Aikin promises to discuss the work of William Drummond in "some future Numbers of this *Reflector*" (II, 86, footnote). The essay on the origin of Medical Science (II, 339A-356) begins with a paragraph discussing the propensity of man to seek the origins of things, but the origin of medicine is obscure, preceding the early Greek records. The first of an unfinished series, the essay is connected to the one on instinct by its style, its survey nature, and a quotation from Lord Kames.

"On the Privileges of a Pedestrian" (II, 228-232) is a personal essay in the traditional manner, with the fictitious correspondent, the personal experience, the genial moralizing. An elderly gentleman chats about himself with a quiet sense of humor. Again he quotes Cowper and again he shows that he knows the medical profession. Though he is "of necessity a pedestrian", the essay is an account of the many advantages of walking, for the pedestrian enjoys the beauties of nature, can study fauna and flora, and is not limited to dusty highways – and walking is good exercise, as "a medical theorist would probably add" (II, 228).

An acquaintance with Dr. Aikin's writings in the *Reflector* confirms the impression one gets from reading the remarks of those who knew him personally. He was a gentleman who did his bit toward enhancing the taste of the public through his sensible and readable essays and who at the same time recorded some of the prevailing sentiments for Hunt's "chronicle for posterity". Though he contributed little to literature or to the development of a genre, he was in tune with the Romantic period which coincided with the last twenty years or so of his life.

Lucy Aikin, who had been writing for magazines and reviews since she was seventeen, contributed one poem to the *Reflector*. In 1810 she had published her first considerable work, *Epistles on Women,* a poem in conventional heroics, but her future was to include novels and some respectable historical works, as well as the memoir of her father. Her books have not been reprinted and only one poem seems to survive in an anthology: "Which Way Does the Wind Blow?" "The Balloon", signed "L.A." (II, 216), was printed on the last page of the third issue of the *Reflector*, possibly because Hunt needed a filler for the page. Her choice of the balloon as a poetic subject may have been suggested by the activities of Sadler, the English aeronaut, who had been making frequent ascents in 1810 and 1812 at Oxford and Cambridge. In August 1811 he made two flights from the Mermaid

Tavern in Hackney, both of more than an hour's duration, both attended by large crowds (including pickpockets), and both vividly described in the press. In form the poem is a sestet; in diction Miss Aikin betrays an embarrassing tendency toward epithets ending in -y. The personification is commonplace; Fancy, Love, and Hope are brought down by Care and Fate, just as a balloon returns to earth with its "breath ethereal" spent. The inspiration in a topical event, the threadbare expression, and the trite didacticism at the end are reasons enough for omission of this poem from any anthology.

B. GEORGE DYER

Dr. Aikin and George Dyer were the oldest of the several contributors to the *Reflector*, both belonging to a generation older than that of Lamb and Hunt. Both were minor men of letters who were ready at all times to break into print, so that a new magazine would be welcome to them. Both were well known if not prominent, and they moved in fairly broad literary circles. Dyer was an old Bluecoat boy, a fact which gave him a common background with the other alumni, but his friendship with Lamb and Coleridge and his personal nature as a "character" have given him an enduring place on the fringes of the circle of the immortals of his day.

No one has written a separate biographical or critical work on Dyer, but he has been given adequate treatment in a chapter of his own in that gold mine, the Lucas biography of Lamb. As to his works, they are voluminous and little more. He was born on March 15, 1755, in Wapping, London, the son of a watchman. Through the benevolence of some ladies he was sent to Christ's Hospital from 1762 to 1774; from there he went to Emanuel College, Cambridge. The next twenty years were occupied in various teaching positions and as tutor in the Robert Robinson family, this last connection resulting in his becoming a Unitarian and writing Robinson's biography, which Wordsworth called one of the best biographies in the language. From 1792 on he lived in London "like a dove in an asp's nest" (to quote Lamb) among

George Dyer

(Painting by Henry Meyer)
(Reproduced by permission of the Syndics of the Fitzwilliam Museum, Cambridge)

the lawyers of Clifford's Inn, writing books, notably one on Cambridge, writing for various periodicals, making indexes and reading proof, searching through libraries, and, in his most memorable aspect, moving through the lives and letters of Coleridge and Lamb. His friends included Priestley, Wakefield, Mrs. Barbauld, Hazlitt, Coleridge, Hunt, Lamb, and many others. To Hunt he was "an angel of the dusty heaven of bookstalls and the British Museum" [6] because he did so much research in public and private libraries throughout England and Scotland. Lamb called him "that common dispenser of benevolence", while to Coleridge he was "my dear brother under many titles".[7] Hunt remembered Dyer's coming to Christ's Hospital to consult books in the library, and Dyer's name appears among the subscribers to Hunt's *Juvenilia*. Dyer's acquaintance with Lamb and Coleridge dates somewhere in the 1790's; Lamb first mentions him in a letter to Coleridge dated July 1, 1796.[8] He met Henry Crabb Robinson around 1799.[9] Just when he met Hunt is not known, but by November 14, 1808, Hunt, who was still at the War Office and editing the *Examiner* at the same time, could write to Marianne and mimic Dyer's hesitant manner of speech, so that he must have known him fairly well.[10] Two years later he was writing for the *Reflector* and composing his last volume of poetry, or "lyric lumber", as Lamb called it.

In later life Dyer became blind. Because of his failing eyesight he walked out of Lamb's house and into the New River in 1823, an incident which Lamb expanded upon for "Amicus Redivivus". Dyer is central in another Lamb essay, "Oxford in the Long Vacation", and he appears in many of the letters and writings of Lamb, Hazlitt, Clarke, Talfourd, Barry Cornwall, and Crabb Robinson. In 1801 Lamb wrote to Coleridge that he would like to put Dyer into a novel when he died, but Dyer outlived Lamb by several years, dying on March 2, 1841, just short of eighty-six

6 *Life*, I, 203.
7 S. E. Winbolt, *The Poetry and Prose of Coleridge, Lamb, and Leigh Hunt* (London, 1920), p. 69.
8 *Letters*, I, 33.
9 *Diary*, I, 39.
10 *Correspondence*, I, 40.

years of age. He lived a somewhat slovenly life, wearing old, ill-fitting, dirty clothing and going about unwashed, unshaven, and underfed until a kindly widow took him in charge and married him in 1825. His naïveté made him the butt of friendly jokes, especially from Lamb, who, among other things, convinced him that Lord Castlereagh was the author of *Waverly*. But Lamb could also write that God "never put a kinder heart into flesh of man than George Dyer's".[11]

The first-hand verbal pictures of Dyer by his contemporaries depict a naïve but kindly man, an unkempt, absent-minded bookworm who wrote much but said little. He was a lovable man, but sadly in need of an influence for orderliness. After reading his 150 pages in the *Reflector*, one may be a little bored, since much of what he writes is no longer of interest. But nowhere do we get the impression of a fumbling, disordered or naïve old man. He is as sensitive to the shortcomings of the society of his day as was Leigh Hunt, yet he is more restrained and detached about them. Sometimes his points are made with less clarity than is expected in expository writing. The abundance of allusions and quotations gives his essays a pedantic cumbersomeness. Footnoting was his weakness, and the many allusions, quotations, and references attest to his bibliographical zeal.

Nine of Dyer's eleven essays in the *Reflector* are signed "An Observer", a common signature among letters to editors, and eight of them are credited to "G. Dyer" in the British Museum copy of the *Reflector*. His essays are strictly informative and in the first person, but they are unrelated to the personal essay. They usually begin with a long generalization (also a Hunt habit) before they launch into their subject matter. Dyer is never polemical but is straightforward and objective, depending for the most part on the "right reason" which he mentions and which he probably acquired, along with some of his other ideas, from Hartley. Two articles by Dyer are neither signed by him nor credited to him by Hunt.

[11] *Letters*, I, 201.

Volume I, Number 1: "On Defects and Abuses in Public Institutions" (Signed "An Observer")
"On Opinions Respecting the English Constitution" (Signed "An Observer")
"On the Catholic Claims" (Unsigned)

Volume I, Number 2: "On the English Constitution (Continued)" (Signed "An Observer")
"On the Easiest Mode of Learning the Greek and Latin Languages, with occasional Strictures on the Greek and Latin Grammars taught in Public Schools" (Signed "An Observer")
"On the Connections and the mutual Assistance of the Arts and Sciences, and the Relation of Poetry to them all" (Signed "An Observer")
"On the Independence of Judges" (Unsigned)

Volume II, Number 3: "Defects in the English Constitution" (Signed "Observer")
Miscellaneous: "On the Bodleian Library" (Signed "An Observer")

Volume II, Number 4: "Why Are There so Few Excellent Poets?" (Signed "An Observer")
"On the best Means of promoting the Fundamental Principles of the English Constitution" (Signed "An Observer")

Dyer's first essay in the *Reflector* (I, 72-81) records some of his observations in schools and hospitals over a period of years and is probably all that was published of a projected work on the prisons and libraries of England.[12] After an introduction giving the etymology of the word *hospital* and a history of such institu-

[12] P. F. Morgan, "A Note on George Dyer", *CLS Bulletin*, #136 (May 1957), p. 159.

tions in England, he lists some of the abuses: Flogging in the public schools, charging entrance fees at free hospitals, intolerable conditions at lunatic hospitals, and the lack of full-time resident physicians at many public institutions. He is pleased to notice the recent abolition of the slave trade and the prevailing spirit of reform.

Dyer's second essay (I, 82-86) turns from defects in public institutions to defects in the English Constitution and is the first of the four *Reflector* essays which Dyer reprinted in book form in 1812 under the title *Four Letters on the English Constitution.* The essay is a collection of opinions about the Constitution, concluding that it is difficult to define because of its latent faults and because of abuse and corruption. The second installment (I, 283-297) traces the growth of the Constitution from the laws of Ethelbert in 561, the Anglo-Norman laws, and those of James I; he draws on such writers as Spelman, Cotton, William Penn, Thomas Paine, and William Blackstone. He maintains that the Constitution is no less real because it is intangible; that, since the Constitution existed before the Church of England, the Church is not part of the Constitution and citizens of all faiths should receive equal protection under it. Kingship is a trust given to one who governs by law under a contract, and the source of power is in the people. Thus Dyer follows Locke in his principle that "As men, we have a natural claim to existence, to liberty, to religion, to whatever comes under the denomination of personal rights; as members of a civil society, to frame the laws by which those rights are to be administered" (I, 287). The "Defects in the English Constitution" (II, 31-43) in the third of the series are two: It is defective in political liberty and in its lack of a clear statement of the prerogatives of the kingly office, an especially timely observation since George III was incapacitated and the Prince of Wales had recently taken over as Prince Regent. The fourth essay (II, 274-298) asserts that he does not wish to involve himself with reform, but since a fundamental principle of the Constitution is civil liberty, the Catholic claims should be recognized, the government should cease encroaching on the liberties of the people by bringing informations *ex officio* for libel, the

Prince Regent should work for the common good rather than joining with self-seeking politicians, and the public should be assured of having full liberty of the press in reporting debates and expressing opinions. Dyer's contribution to the constitutional debates of 1812 probably caused few ripples in that already choppy sea upon which stronger crafts were being launched every day. Like Dyer, the essays are very mild, lost as he was amidst personalities more forceful, more willing to plunge into the rough waters of controversy.

Dyer's two unsigned articles, "On the Catholic Claims" (I, 174-207) in the first issue and "On the Independence of Judges" (II, 21-25) in the third are closely related to the Constitution articles, with many similarities that clearly indicate that Dyer is the author. In only one respect do these articles differ from those with his "Observer" signature: They speak with an air of authority and assume a firmness made possible, perhaps, by anonymity. But the diction, style, and ideas are Dyer's. "On the Catholic Claims" begins with a paragraph very similar to the opening of "On the Defects and Abuses in Public Institutions". Both speak of improvements in society such as reform and the abolition of the slave trade, and they are identical in style and tone. Two phrases near the beginning of the article sound like the mild-mannered Dyer of other articles. He writes that his remarks are submitted with diffidence and he modestly asserts that "the cause of civil and religious liberty cannot be materially injured by the occasional deficiency of its advocates" (I, 174). The plethora of footnotes and citations is a Dyer characteristic. Favorite words and expressions tie this article to the rest of Dyer's contributions: "the welfare of the rising religion cemented with their blood" is a figure of speech repeated in the last of the Constitution series: "Civil and religious liberty . . . is the true cement of the English Constitution" (I, 179; II, 295). Civil liberty is the foundation upon which he bases the validity of the Catholic claims in this article and which is also stated in the final article of the serial. Finally, Dyer has a fondness for the word *nugatory*. In the article "Defects of the English Constitution" he uses the phrase "The political liberty of which constitution, in short, must be nugatory"

(II, 35); in the present article he uses the word in the same manner three times.

The same word is one of the connecting links with the unsigned article in the third issue, "On the Independence of Judges". Though the article is much shorter than most of Dyer's essays, it is Dyer in style and content and is actually an expansion of a part of his final article of the serial which said that judges and lawyers have been encroaching on the liberty of the people, especially in public libels, because of an obligation to the Crown. But Dyer says the impartiality of a judge comes from his character, not his office, and the public must depend upon juries for complete impartiality.

Except for the short piece in the third issue on the Bodleian Library (II, 209-211), the rest of Dyer's essays concern the fine arts. In the second issue (I, 332-345) he proposes "the Easiest Mode of Learning the Greek and Latin Languages". He advises the student to begin with Greek because it is the older and sweeter of the two languages. Pronunciation should come first, after which one should learn the grammar and vocabulary simultaneously. "The Connection and the Mutual Assistance of the Arts and Sciences, and the Relation of Poetry to Them All" (I, 346-360) has a good summary of the article in its title, although his short discussion of imagination is interesting since the subject was a favorite with the Romantics. "It is the province of invention, the supreme faculty of poetic genius, to discover and to collect", but "it is the province of imagination, the very soul of poetry, to bring near distant objects, to unite them into one form, and to give them a glow, as from a painter's hand" (I, 355). He concludes with the Hartleyan idea that "All knowledge is derived from the association of ideas; and man's knowledge is in proportion to his number of ideas" (I, 360).

Dyer asserts that there are "few excellent poets" (II, 249-274) because the motives which make people write often destroy excellence, for "from muddy springs flow muddy waters" – a phrase which, curiously enough, is found in Shelley's poem, "England in 1819", as "mud from a muddy spring". "The principal reason, why . . . there have existed so few excellent poets, is, that the spring and source do not arise in majesty and true greatness" (II, 273). "Genius", he says, "is the towering eagle that soars high, sails on the whirlwind, and sees and feels vast things" (II, 270). Some poets lack the vast capability of associating ideas and the flow of imagination; poetic genius, to Dyer, is not only the vivid perception and sensibility and the ability to associate ideas in the imagination, but also the flash or illumination that comes from nowhere and ignites poetic genius, a combination of the explainable and the unexplainable, of the received impressions plus divine inspiration.

Considered in relation to other periodical essayists of his day, Dyer is "milk and water" when compared to the acidity and acrimony of a Jeffrey or even a Gilchrist; he is not interested in an argument and he avoids the rough and tumble arena of the controversial essay. His articles lack the derogation of others and the exaltation of self so typical of the critical writers of his day, and at the same time have little of the strength which could be there, even without vituperation. In the *Reflector* period Dyer was already middle-aged, his habits were established, and he was not likely to succumb to the Romantic tendency for the subjective or the self-revelatory, the confessional habit that was to become a watermark of the personal essays of Lamb, Hazlitt, DeQuincey, and Hunt. Those days were dawning, and Dyer was not only of a different temperament, but of a different age.

C. OCTAVIUS GILCHRIST

Octavius Graham Gilchrist is unique among literary men: he was a grocer. He was one of the fifteen children of Sterling Gilchrist, an army surgeon, and one of his brothers, A. R. Gilchrist, was an artist. He was born at Twickenham on March 11, 1779. He was educated at Magdalen College, Oxford, but he left without taking a degree in order to help a relative, Alderman Joseph Robinson of Stamford, in his grocery business, which he afterwards carried on himself. The Society of Antiquaries elected him a Fellow in 1803. In 1804 he married Elizabeth Nowlan, daughter of a merchant of Wapping, London. No children are mentioned in his obituary. His short life was spent in Stamford, where he knew John Scott and John Drakard of the *Stamford News*, but he had friends in London, too, including William Gifford and John Taylor. He knew Barron Field, probably through Gifford, but he was evidently not in London enough to become associated with the Lamb or Hunt circles, which were oriented toward Christ's Hospital and Cambridge. The *Monthly Mirror* for August 1810 published a "Memoir of Octavius Gilchrist, Esq. F.A.S., with a portrait" in which he speaks of "our friend Hunt" whose "memoir" had appeared in the *Mirror* a few months previously.

His home in Stamford was a cheerful, comfortable place where hearty meals, music, poetry, and friendliness prevailed. At least one impoverished poet found an oasis there: John Clare, the peasant poet of Northamptonshire. A few years after Gilchrist's death Clare wrote to Taylor, "Poor Gilchrist was the only man of letters in this neighborhood, and now he has left it a desert." [13] Gilchrist suffered for a long time from consumption, which caused his death in 1823. The next year his extensive library was sold at auction.

Gilchrist published privately a volume of *Rhymes* in 1805, but his reputation as an antiquary is based largely on his 1808 edition of the poems of Richard Corbet, Bishop of Norwich (1582-1635), and his work in research and criticism connected with old plays. In the same year he published a refutation of statements by prominent Shakespearean critics regarding the enmity of Ben Jonson toward Shakespeare. A reviewer said that the essay contained "much acuteness of research", but that it could display just as much ingenuity without using such harsh language.[14] Late in 1810 he contributed his one article to the *Reflector*. He furnished Gifford with numerous notes for his work on Jonson and his edition of Massinger's plays, and he touched off a controversy with his uncomplimentary remarks about William Lisle Bowles in the October 1820 *Quarterly*. Perhaps his most influential writing was his article introducing John

[13] John William and Anne Tibble, *John Clare* (New York, 1932), p. 340.
[14] *Gentleman's Magazine*, LXXIX (January, 1809), 53.

Octavius Gilchrist

(Painting by Lonsdale, engraving by Freeman)
(Published in "Monthly Mirror" for August, 1810)

Clare to the world in the January 1820 *London Magazine*. He is generally credited with the very favorable review of Clare's *Poems* in the *Quarterly* that same year. His most extensive project was a fifteen-volume collection of old English plays, but the project was abandoned on the publication of Charles Wentworth Dilke's *Old English Plays* (1814-1816).

Volume I, Number 1: "On the Origin of Shakespeare's Tempest"
(Signed "Octavius Gilchrist")

The first issue of the *Reflector* contained Gilchrist's only contribution, "On the Origin of Shakespeare's Tempest" (I, 100-107). Gilchrist's connection with Hunt can probably be traced through Barron Field, who mentions their friendship in a *Reflector* article (I, 109), and Field may have brought the article to Hunt's attention, since it is the kind that fits in well with the standards outlined in the Prospectus. The article is one of the two in the four issues of the magazine having an undisguised signature, the other being the "C. Lamb" on "A Farewell to Tobacco".

The article begins with the common pseudo-epistolary style by addressing "Mr. Reflector", and its occasional use of the first person pronoun gives it a somewhat informal air. Since a superfluity of observations on Shakespeare has already worn the path rather thin, he says he will pursue a less hackneyed subject, the sources. His introductory remarks on the development of comedy in the sixteenth century show that he has been working on Dodsley's *Old Plays*, and he says that collection should have included *Mucedorus*, a play of uncertain authorship first published in 1598. He has also been reading an unpublished pamphlet by the Shakespeare scholar, Malone, on the sources of *The Tempest*, and his own research enables him to add two points:

> Collins the poet, had a romance called *Aurelio and Isabella*, which furnished the loves of Ferdinand and Miranda; and the "conceitede comedie of *Mucedorus*," perhaps, supplied some of the features of the monster Caliban. (I, 103).

The first point is ambiguous, since he means that Collins was apparently acquainted with a play by that name, but this was a misunderstanding that has been disproved in the *Variorum* edition of *The Tempest*: the old Spanish play, published in Italian, Spanish, French, and English in 1588, has nothing in common with Shakespeare's play. The *Variorum* has nothing to say of *Mucedorus*, and Gilchrist is probably closer to the truth when he says, "Both, most probably, had their origin in the uncouth personages of the rustic pageants" (I, 105), the drolls which he mentions earlier in his article. The same suggestion appears in the Arden Shakespeare: "It is not absolutely impossible that Shakespeare may have known some old play on the lines of *Mucedorus* which may have contributed something to the total pattern of *The Tempest*." [15] Gilchrist quotes passages from *Mucedorus* to show resemblances in tone and idea to one passage in *The Tempest* and to illustrate its Shakespearean style. What he says then is true:

> The following passages . . . manifest the hand of a master, and will be read with pleasure even though they should fail to prove that, in the character and language of his "servant-monster," Shakespeare owed any obligations to the "comedie of *Mucedorus*." (I, 106).

Admittedly the passage he quotes is worthy of Shakespeare, but since it was published when Shakespeare was already a well-known poet and playwright, the "university wit" to whom it is credited may have been imitating Shakespeare. But Gilchrist is not attempting to prove anything; he is only pointing out resemblances which would seem to indicate that Shakespeare had that popular comedy in mind when he wrote his play.

Since the *Variorum* edition does not mention *Mucedorus* as a possible source and other speculations are quoted and refuted, the editors were probably unaware of Gilchrist's article. Gilchrist himself was rather tentative in his declarations, and the resemblances he points out are interesting even though they prove nothing in the way of borrowings, conscious or otherwise. Gilchrist's literary style in the article is somewhat unsatisfactory, lacking the clarity of his later writings and the conviction of his controversial essays. Perhaps the most unsatisfactory aspect of

[15] Frank Kermode (ed.), *The Tempest* (Cambridge, 1954), p. lxiv.

his *Tempest* article is the inaccuracy of his quotations, the carelessness in transcribing them, sometimes changing whole lines. But the essay is interesting and provocative, even if it does not come up to his articles on Jonson and Clare.

D. THE ANONYMOUS CONTRIBUTORS

For many years before and after the *Reflector* period, the practice of publishing letters and articles without the names of the authors was the rule rather than the exception, a practice which gave the writers freedom to criticize and protection from physical and legal retaliation by those whom they criticized. Libel laws were not what they are today, and apparently writers' vanity did not include seeing their names in print. Many of the better writers were known in spite of the omission of the signature, such as Southey in the *Quarterly Review* and Hunt in the *Examiner* and *Reflector*. Although all anonymous writing was not vituperative, anonymity afforded a temptation and an opportunity for personal, unfair, partisan, and malicious criticism, and the criticism of Hunt and Keats in the Cockney School articles by Lockhart in *Blackwood's* is a notorious example.

This predilection for anonymity is often an insurmountable obstacle in the way of one who would identify the authors of periodical articles. The reprinting of an article in a writer's collected works, internal evidence such as similar passages in correspondence, or the casual mention of an article in correspondence or memoirs are of great help. Only two of the 112 items in the four issues of the *Reflector* carry the names of their authors, the essay by Gilchrist and the poem by Lamb. Many lack a signature of any kind or have a symbol or pseudonym which may or may not have had any connection with the writer. One practice was to use a name of Greek or Latin derivation appropriate to the particular article, such as Scholefield's "Philo-Tragicus" for his article on Greek and English tragedy and Lamb's "Pensilis" (hanging) for his "On the Inconveniences Resulting from Being Hanged". Barron Field chose to use three daggers in the *Reflector*, three asterisks and sometimes his initials in the *Examiner*.

Dyer used the hackneyed "An Observer" while Aikin, Barnes, Mitchell, and Scholefield usually used initials, though they are not consistent. Hunt's "indicator" or printer's hand was too well known from its weekly appearance in the *Examiner* to be a disguise, and this familiar pointing finger is affixed to most, but not all, of his contributions in the *Reflector*.

The problem of identifying the *Reflector* articles is helped considerably by Hunt's pencil notations in the British Museum copy of the magazine as well as his remarks in his *Autobiography*. With these aids about 80% of the articles can be identified with some confidence. But too often Hunt gives help where no help is needed, as in the case of the signed articles, and omits it where it would be most useful. Identifying the fourteen items by Lamb is no problem, for Lamb had reprinted twelve of them during his lifetime. The articles signed "An Observer" are credited to Dyer, but four of them appeared in book form in 1812 and two unsigned articles by Dyer are not credited to him by Hunt. Two of Aikin's articles have been reprinted. None of the articles by Field, Gilchrist, Mitchell, or Scholefield have been reprinted, but an article and a poem by Barnes are included in the appendix to the Hudson biography of Barnes.

In his *Autobiography* Hunt gives a list of contributors to the *Reflector*: "Lamb, Dyer, Barnes, Mitchell, the Greek Professor Scholefield (all Christ Hospital men), together with Dr. Aikin and his family, wrote in it." [16] The British Museum copy adds Barron Field, Gilchrist, and Lucy Aikin, but it does not indicate which essays are by Mitchell or Scholefield. The "M" and the "S" affixed to certain articles, plus internal evidence, point to Mitchell and Scholefield, but both wrote others as well. Scholefield wrote at least two more, and conversely, two of the items signed "S" could not have been written by him. Thus Hunt was of some help, but he could have been more thorough in his help. Possibly he made his notations in the bound volume of the *Reflector* many years after publication, when he could no longer remember who wrote all of the articles. At any rate, no systematic evidence, such an account book listing payments for articles, seems to exist.

[16] *Autobiography*, p. 214.

Ninety-one items in the four issues of the *Reflector* can be attributed with confidence to certain writers on the basis of external and internal evidence; of the remaining twenty-one items, three can be attributed to writers (Robert Hunt and Thomas Moore) on the basis of likelihood and a provisional guess. The other twelve full-length articles and six short pieces cannot be identified. Some of the twenty-one items discussed in this chapter are relatively unimportant, being ephemerae, space-fillers, letters from readers, and the like. But some are constructive and well worth reading, and a few inspire speculation that they may have come from the pen of someone of more than passing interest – Hunt's brother Robert, for example.

No one has mentioned Robert Hunt as a contributor to the *Reflector* and perhaps he did not write for it. But it would indeed be strange if he did not. He was associated with John and Leigh Hunt on the *Examiner* as a reporter of exhibitions. Like everyone else he probably needed money; and while he may have been doing some engraving and painting, the limited information about Robert Hunt does not reveal his primary source of income. He may have been on a salary from the *Examiner*, but in many weeks his offerings were very short or totally missing.

Hunt mentions Robert only a few times in the early pages of the *Autobiography* and not at all after about 1807, so that information about him is limited. He was born in America around 1774, about four years before Mrs. Hunt took her family to England. He went to a day-school at Finchley, and he must have been a husky boy, for Hunt tells of his walking a hundred miles in two days and trotting beside a horse all the way from Finchley to Pimlico. Robert Hunt studied engraving with Robert Thew, a self-taught artist who became historical engraver to the Prince of Wales, but since Thew died in 1802, Robert must have been on his own by the time Leigh was looking for a vocation. In the discarded chapters of *Lord Byron and Some of His Contemporaries*, Hunt gives some information about Robert:

I next became pupil to my brother Robert, who had studied engraving under Mr. Thew, an eminent artist of that time; but I do not remember even taking the graver in hand. My brother himself was ill fitted by temperament for this sedentary and poring art, which picks and gnaws its way through the hard metal; though, for eye, I will venture to say that he was unsurpassed by anyone.[17]

Robert did enough painting to have an exhibit at the Royal Academy, so that he probably studied there under the sponsorship of his uncle, its president; but his paintings, including one of his brother John, have disappeared.

In 1806-1807 he did some of the illustrations for Leigh Hunt's *Classic Tales* and the design for the title page, but his name appears under them as painter and designer, not as engraver. While he may not have succeeded as an artist, Robert could write about engravings and paintings with intelligence, discrimination, and the Huntian air of authority, and he did so in the *Examiner*.

Robert Hunt was about thirty-four when the *Examiner* first appeared, and his "Fine Arts" column, signed with his initials, began in the summer of 1808 with a report on "Blake's Edition of Blair's Grave".[18] He continued to write for the *Examiner*, somewhat irregularly, as late as 1826. Ironically, he is now remembered chiefly through his adverse criticism of Blake, in his September 17, 1809, account of "Mr. Blake's Exhibition". Blake confused him completely; he was "an unfortunate lunatic, whose personal inoffensiveness secures him from confinement", and his pictures were "unintelligible allegory".[19] When Robert married Priscilla John on April 11, 1811, the *Examiner* printed the announcement on the back page with other vital statistics. They had at least one child, Mary Cornelia, whose married name was Rushworth. Years later Thornton Hunt wrote of his uncle Robert as "an artist, utterly devoid of any natural talent, except for digestion, married to a pattern of conjugal worth and charitable affection . . . the thriftless, thoughtless, bookless, homely non-artist".[20] When Robert was in distress in 1848, Leigh Hunt applied to the crown for assistance for him, and he was nominated

[17] *Leigh Hunt's Autobiography, The Earliest Sketches*, pp. 35-36.

[18] *Examiner* (1808), p. 509.

[19] *Examiner* (1809), p. 605. See also David V. Erdman, "Blake's 'Nest of Villains' ", *K-SJ*, II (1953), 61-71.

[20] *Leigh Hunt and His Circle*, p. 361.

Robert Hunt in 1819

(Drawing by John Linnel, 1819)
(Copyright, National Portrait Gallery)

by Queen Victoria to a vacancy in Charterhouse, the home for aged poor near Smithfield, where he died on August 19, 1850, aged seventy-six years. His death went unnoticed in the periodicals and letters and memoirs of other writers do not mention his passing. Except that he had a well-known brother and had written critically of Blake, he might never have existed.

Among the anonymous articles in the *Reflector*, two were very likely written by Robert Hunt:

Volume I, Number 2: "On the Responsibility of Members of Academies of Arts, and in Vindication of the late Professor Barry from the Aspersions of the Edinburgh Review" (Unsigned)

Volume II, Number 3: "On the Talents of Frey and Piranesi, Considered with Reference to the State of Italian Engraving in the Century which Preceded Them" (Signed "Philographicus")

The long titles and the prepositional beginnings are typical of essays of the day and quite unlike the terse titles to which Robert was limited in the *Examiner*. The first article, undated, was published in July 1811; the second is dated August 1811 and was published in October. If we are to trust these dates, Robert would have had plenty of time to write them, since he wrote nothing for the *Examiner* from August 18 to September 29, 1811.

As its title indicates, the first article (I, 388-408) is in two parts. The first half is a dialogue between Academicus and Crito on the efficacy of Academies; the second is an account of the expulsion of James Barry from the Royal Academy. The article is part of the reaction to two *Edinburgh Review* articles by R. P. Knight, who reviewed the recently published *Works and Life of James Barry*, and both Lamb and Leigh Hunt gave considerable attention to Barry in their *Reflector* articles. The second article, on Frey and Piranesi, the engravers (II, 187-195), is addressed to the editor, and it invites Mr. Reflector's comments as to why two fine engravers should appear in Italy in the eighteenth century after a century when Italy had no competent engravers at all. After a short opening generalization, the writer gives biographies of the two men and discusses the art of Piranesi with the air of one who knows whereof he speaks.

The writing in both articles is clear and detached, revealing an insight into the niceties and the mechanics of engraving and an appreciation of fine art; it is rather mild in tone, often poetic in expression, and replete with quotations from Voltaire and various poets. Occasional verbal links connect the essays with Robert Hunt's writing in the *Examiner*. For example, the first article condemns the injurious system and the spirit of corporate pride in the academies, and his December 15, 1811, *Examiner* article comments on the "selfishness of system" in academies and the "selfish views" of individuals. A link between the two *Reflector* articles is their concern with artists who have been expelled from academies, Barry and Soane from the Royal Academy and Piranesi from the Roman academy. In one respect these articles differ from those in the *Examiner*: Robert's *Reflector* articles are never dogmatic, opinionated, or vituperative, as they sometimes became in the *Examiner*, but perhaps in the more dignified surroundings of a quarterly magazine he felt he could forget the *Examiner's* fiercely independent spirit for a time.

Certainly these resemblances and conjectures do not prove that Robert Hunt wrote the articles. But on the many grounds for believing that he did write for the *Reflector*, these articles are the most likely products of his pen.

Since reform was one of the aims of the *Reflector*, about a fourth of its articles concern politics, and the authorship of most of them can be established. The authors of three comparatively unimportant political items are still unknown.

Volume I, Number 2: "Church and Constitution" (Unsigned)
Miscellaneous: "A Libel Discovered"
(Signed "Indagator")

Volume II, Number 3: Miscellaneous: "The Patriot's Almanack" (Signed "Politician")

The first article in the second issue of the *Reflector*, "Church and Constitution" (I, 249-255), is an innocuous item for so prominent a spot, but the two subjects of its title were frequently in the news because the unwritten Constitution led to a variety of interpretations. This article is concerned with definitions, interpreting the church in terms of the national or established church and the Constitution as a set of precedents plus the three branches of government "which together constitute the supreme power" (I, 255). The subject matter suggests that George Dyer, who wrote briefly about the Catholic claims and at length on the Constitution, may have been the writer. He quotes Bishop Spelman, and Dyer quotes him four times in his articles. But the style of this unknown writer is quite different from that of Dyer, a straightforward style with few quotations and no footnotes at all.

"A Libel Discovered" (I, 473-477) is signed "Indagator", meaning one who searches, a fairly common name for signatures on letters to editors. This short, clever satire is directed against the attorney general, Sir Vicary Gibbs, and his zeal in bringing "informations" for libel. Indagator calls his attention to a publication whose writers and publishers should be prosecuted for libel against the government because it advocates peace, forgiveness, love for one's neighbors, and moderation in the pursuit of money, all things which are "a perpetual libel on our manners and institutions" (I, 475). If such mischievous precepts were to be adopted by the majority of the country, the government would not be able to "carry on those martial operations from which we are at present deriving so much honour and advantage"; therefore, the attorney general is being very lenient when he pursues "such petty game as newspaper essayists on the military discipline of flogging" (I, 476). The publication is, of course, the Bible. Ridicule is a sharp weapon, often more effective than the blunt frontal attack that Hunt habitually used.

"The Patriot's Almanack" (II, 206-207) purports to be a prospectus for a political or patriotic almanac but is actually a vehicle for a mild but well-camouflaged attack upon the government. The almanac would consist of a calendar of important historical events such as the treason trial of Hardy and Took, whose acquittal is celebrated with a dinner each year; a supplement containing information about the boroughs and their voters, the national debt, the poor, the pensioners, and sinecures would follow. This short item is of special interest since it may have been written by Thomas Moore, who wrote to Hunt in September 1811 about a "fragment" which he had written for the *Reflector* and which he called "wickedly political". "Some of the allusions have now lost their hold", he wrote, "but you shall see it, and perhaps something may, with your assistance, be yet made of it." [21] The item is certainly political, though hardly wicked, and although it may not be the one referred to by Moore, it comes close to his description.

Volume I, Number 1: "On the Pernicious Effects of Methodism in our Foreign Possessions" (Signed "A Member of the Established Church, February 23, 1810")

In 1808 Hunt published a series of anti-Methodist articles in the *Examiner* which he brought out in book form the next year under the title *An Attempt to Shew the Folly and Danger of Methodism.* In it Hunt violently attacked the Methodists, saying among other things that "A religion, like Methodism, is not fit for a free nation." Hunt was concerned with Methodism in England, whereas the unknown writer of the *Reflector* article (I, 35-43) is concerned with the attempts of the Methodists to spread their "fanaticism" in the East and West Indies.

The essay is heated, biased, and intolerant, denouncing a group of Methodists who have tried to convert the Negroes in Jamaica and who have been restrained by the government. While he agrees with the injunction to take the gospel into all lands, the writer insists that this should be done only under the jurisdiction

[21] Moore, p. 393.

of the British government and the established church. The Methodists can send missionaries to Africa if they wish, but not to a British colony. The missionaries' sponsors, sectarian Methodist and Baptist societies, and a periodical, the *Christian Observer,* which favors the missionary effort, are particularly censured, while the writer praises the *Anti-Jacobin Review* for its opposition to the effort. John Larpent, the inspector of plays, is one government official who is looked upon with disfavor, since he insists that the Methodists are harmless and refuses to approve a play which has a preacher in it. The style of this unidentified writer is unlike that of any of the identified writers in the *Reflector.*

Volume I, Number 1: Miscellaneous: "Character of Charles I" (Unsigned)

Volume I, Number 2: "Remarkable Passages from the Memoirs of the Marshal de Bassompierre" (Unsigned)
"Remarks on Hume's History of England" (Signed "Camilla")

Volume II, Number 4: "On the Favourites of Princes" (Unsigned)
"On Contempt of Popularity" (Unsigned)

Five of the anonymous articles in the *Reflector* are related to one another through content, references, and general attitude. The works of Bassompierre connect the first two; the first, third, and fourth are refutations of statements in David Hume's *History of England* (1778); the fourth and fifth are closely related by style and by internal evidence.

"Character of Charles I" (I, 245-248) contradicts Hume's complimentary picture of Charles' character and disposition. It quotes an account of the embassy of the French diplomat, Francois de Bassompierre, to the English court in 1626 to settle the question of the Catholic servants of Queen Henrietta. Hume, says this writer, presents Charles in a way which is "most adapted to excite sympathy and attachment" by de-emphasizing his early characteristics of "wilfulness, precipitation, and the pride of royalty" and by emphasizing his later character "when long calamities had softened his temper" (I, 245). The essayist himself betrays an anti-Catholic bias in one comment on Henrietta: She was "bigottedly attached to her religion" (I, 246). The second article (I, 256-266) consists of seven incidents from Bassompierre's memoirs (published in Cologne in 1665) tied together with commentary which often seems pointed toward the Prince Regent. In commenting on the profligacy of Henry IV of France this writer says, "It does not enhance our ideas of the wisdom and dignity of a monarch of fifty-five, that the discourse of pandars should be encouraged in his presence" (I, 257). The next article in the same issue (I, 266-273) is again devoted to Hume's *History*, asserting that this popular historical work is filled with inaccuracies, omissions, and bias, and the refutation of this bias is a connecting link with the other articles. The writer points out several examples of Hume's prejudice in favor of the crown and against the aristocracy; Hunt expressed the same sentiment in speaking of Walter Scott's "innate and trusting reverence for thrones and dominations" in a footnote to "Feast of the Poets" (II, 316). Again some of the remarks can be taken as editorial by inference, a strong hint in favor of virtues lacking in the present administration. "On the Favourites of Princes" (II, 217-222) continues the criticism of the same bias in Hume, this time citing his defense of Edward's relationship with Piers Gaveston – again the implied criticism of the Prince Regent, some of whose favorites were not well thought of, to say the least. Royal disregard for public opinion and similarities in literary style tie this article closely with the next one in the same issue, "On Contempt of Popularity" (II, 223-227), which concludes that anyone "who is indifferent to the approbation of his fellow-citizens is no fit member of a free state" and asks, "If the favourites of the people have sometimes been profligate, what have been those of kings and princes?" (II, 227, 226). This criticism of the Prince Regent's disregard of public opinion was a common one in the opposition press; Hunt repeated it in his "Retrospect of Public Affairs" in the third *Reflector*.

While the authorship of these articles cannot be established with any certainty, one is tempted to think that Thomas Mitchell may have been the author, for two reasons. First, none of the essays in the first two issues carried his initial, though he may have written the brief item signed "Metriculus" in the second issue. In all, only six items bear the signature "M" and his full-length articles do not appear until the fourth issue. These anonymous articles would have given him better representation in the early issues, and as an employee of a crown diplomat he may have felt that his employer would disapprove of his criticism of the Prince Regent. Second, the strongest evidence that Mitchell is the author lies in his interest in French memoirs, as shown by his review of the letters of Mlle de l'Espinasse. But this evidence is inconclusive, too, since others were reading and writing about French publications also – Hunt and Barnes, for example.

Volume II, Number 3: "Reflections on the late Attempt to alter the Act of Toleration" (Signed "Civis")
"On the different Grounds of Religious Persecution" (Unsigned)
Miscellaneous: "Anecdotes from the Memoirs of La Noue, named Bras-de-Fer, a Distinguished Leader of the Protestant Party in France: By Moses Amirault" (Unsigned)

The three articles on toleration in the third issue of the *Reflector* stem from a May 9, 1811, bill introduced by Lord Sidmouth, who, as Henry Addington, cut such a sorry figure in leading his country earlier in the decade (and who, incidentally, was instrumental in getting Leigh Hunt his job at the War Office). The bill was introduced about five months before this issue appeared, and Hunt gave it some attention in his "Retrospect" (II, 183-184). The bill was supposed to prevent what Sidmouth claimed were violations of the Act of Toleration, but the bill met with such strong opposition from so many prominent members of Parliament that it was thrown out on its second reading twelve days later. The "Reflections" (II, 14-21) point out that Sidmouth's political wisdom was never very great, that the word "toleration" means "endurance of what is disapproved", and that until everyone has a "full right of choice in religion" and toleration is "superseded by equality", British liberty will be defective (II, 20-21). "On the Different Grounds of Religious Persecution" (II, 52-61) and the short piece based on the memoirs of La Noue (II, 200-203), who lived from 1531 to 1591, are undoubtedly by the same author, for they are concerned with the motives for persecution and may have been suggested by Sidmouth's bill. The unknown writer uses the Inquisition, the persecution of the Hugenots, and the persecutions by Queen Mary as his examples and says that since zeal is by nature intolerant, civil and religious liberty in the present period should be guarded with care. These articles are mild editorials, too mild to have been written by Hunt. The author uses the words *sect* and *sectary* rather often (they are the subject of an etymological essay elsewhere in the *Reflector*), but he uses a more unusual word, *oppugn*, and its derivatives three times, and this is a word which appears in the *Reflector* in the writings of Barron Field. While this is not proof of authorship, this verbal idiosyncrasy points to Field as a possibility.

Volume II, Number 3: "Cursory Remarks on the Proper Objects in the Education of the Middle and Lower Classes; and on the Most Effectual Mode of Obtaining Them" (Signed "R.F.E.")

On the Table of Contents page in the second issue of the *Reflector* Hunt inserted several paragraphs of notes addressed "To Correspondents", one of which read: "R. F. E., on the Proper Objects in the Education of the Middle and Lower Classes, in the next number." The nineteen-page article duly made its appearance in the third issue (II, 160-179), signed with the writer's initials. Even if Hunt knew the name of the author, he did not reveal it, nor does anyone with these initials appear in standard biographical reference works. However, R.F.E. lived in Birmingham and wrote two letters to the *Examiner* during 1811.[22] His letters reveal a sense of humor, an interest in national events, and the breadth of his reading, but nothing of any connection with education.

R.F.E. may not have an educator, but he knew educational systems and what had been written about them. He was strictly a utilitarian, saying that "Education should qualify mankind not for talking, but for action" (II, 166), although he conceded that a little grammar would be useful. Penmanship and calculation are the subjects most useful to the middle class; after that they should study whatever enables them to employ their leisure well: biography, natural history, and "stories which exhibit life as it is; which represent virtuous man as struggling with misfortune and which, by engaging pity on the side of virtue, induce the practice of it" (II, 172). R.F.E. was somewhat of a sociologist in asserting that better education would help to reduce crime. He concluded that the public form of education was superior to the private and should be expanded on a national scale, and he closed his article with a suggestion to the Prince Regent that he commence his reign by giving attention to a system of national education.

Volume II, Number 3: "On the Advantages of the Present Age" (Signed "E.B.H.")

One of the best satires in the *Reflector* was written by someone identified only by his initials, and the possibility of its author's name becoming known is remote, since no one of those initials appears in publication lists or biographical reference books. "On the Advantages of the Present Age" (II, 156-160) is a short and well-written survey of England in early 1812 with an ostensibly optimistic view but actually directing attention to the disadvantages of the age. When the writer is melancholy from reading about corruption and sinecures, he turns to the *Morning Post,* the strongly pro-administration paper, to read about the best of

22 *Examiner* (1811), pp. 172-173 and 520.

kings and constitutions. He is amazed and gratified to observe that the government can be run without a king and without common sense, that a general can obtain a glorious victory by running away, and so on. He compliments Rowland Hill's "improved" style of preaching, meaning just the opposite, of course. Riches are a passport to good society. Therefore people should look on the bright side of things and forget such trifles as the mismanagement of an expedition, a few sinecures, or the increase of the national debt. The article is a sharp commentary on the times, a gentle satire of which anyone, even Hunt, could have been proud.

Volume I, Number 2: Miscellaneous: "To the Editor of the Reflector" (On Porson and the Anapest) (Signed "Metriculus")

Volume II, Number 4: Miscellaneous: "On the Words *Sect* and *Sectary*" (Unsigned)
"Old Maids" (Signed "O.M.")

The short letter which concludes the second issue of the *Reflector* (I, 485-486) was written by someone who knew his classics and Greek versification thoroughly. His letter is a contradiction of a remark in the February 1810 *Quarterly Review* accusing the great Porson of an oversight, and he defends Porson in his detailed explanation of the particular verse and shows that Porson's accusers are themselves guilty of oversight. "Let us pause a little, and reflect, before we allow the stability of Porson's reputation to be shaken by young Editors and perhaps younger Reviewers" (I, 486). If it were not for the reference to young editors and reviewers, the letter might have been written by Scholefield, age twenty-two, or Mitchell, age twenty-eight, as both were students at Cambridge when the letter was written. As it is, the little item must remain unidentified, but Hunt was not one to pass up an opportunity to contradict something in the *Quarterly*.

The brief item discussing the words *sect* and *sectary* (II, 437-440) may have been suggested to the writer by their frequent use in some of the *Reflector* articles. According to this writer, the words now apply to groups outside of the national religious establishment and imply that being a dissenter is morally criminal. The title and the subject resemble an earlier note by Dr. Aikin on the word *humour* (II, 197-198), and his interest in etymology and semantics would justify an assumption that this is another of his unsigned contributions.

"Old Maids" (II, 501-503) is an essay which sounds very much like Charles Lamb, but no external evidence exists which would support such an attribution. The writer sympathizes with ladies who are over thirty, are still called "Miss", and are embarrassed by their circumstances. To insure their happiness, they should adopt the title "Mrs." when they have reached the hopeless age, and fathers should give these "old maids" a marriage portion so that they can be independent. The signature "O.M." is intended to indicate that the article was written by an Old Maid, and Lamb's sister was an old maid with dim hopes, chances, or desires of marriage. Lamb was certainly a thoughtful and considerate man, blessed with a unique sense of humor; the wry but sympathetic humor and the tongue-in-cheek suggestions all remind one of Lamb. But if Lamb were the author, he – and others – would have reprinted the article, for it is better than one or two of the short *Reflector* pieces that he acknowledged. Its unknown author was thus one who could, at least once, turn out something worthy of Lamb, and that is no small compliment.

Volume II, Number 2: "Athens and England" (Signed "S")
"On the Change of Structure Induced on Animals by Domestication" (Signed "S")

The two articles signed "S" in the final issue have already been discussed in the chapter on Scholefield. Though they are signed in the same manner as five of Scholefield's essays, Scholefield was not their author, and Hunt failed to indicate their authorship in the British Museum copy of the *Reflector*.

"Athens and England" (II, 419-428) is an editorial which compares conditions in the two periods and draws a lesson from history. While not polemical, its author is clearly a reformist, echoing the usual complaints about the Perceval administration and advocating constitutional reform. The author was a classical scholar, and the intellectual basis of the article reflects the orientation of the *Reflector* toward an intellectual audience and its purpose of reinforcing the *Examiner*'s efforts for reform. The scholarly reformist may have been Barnes or Mitchell or someone outside the Hunt coterie.

"On the Change of Structure Induced on Animals by Domestication" (II, 380-387) resembles some of Dr. Aikin's writings in the area of instinct and perception and in the catholicity of subjects which interested him. And Dr. Aikin could have been a friend of Mungo Park. On the other hand, the style does not resemble Aikin's and brevity was not one of his virtues. Therefore, the article is probably a contribution from a *Reflector* reader whose name may or may not have begun with "S", a contributor who will very likely remain anonymous.

The unidentified articles in the *Reflector* will remain an intriguing mystery and a challenge to researchers, although many of them are inconsequential ephemera which would not justify the expenditure of effort. However, because the pseudonyms may hide someone of more than passing interest, one would like to know who "O.M." and the scholar-reformist "S" were, and proof that "Philo-Graphicus" is Robert Hunt would make a worthwhile footnote for Leigh Hunt specialists. R.F.E. can probably be identified in time because of his three initials and his residence in Birmingham. Except for the attraction of an unsolved problem, the other anonymous contributions are of little importance – further comments on reform, etymology, excerpts from memoirs, coming painfully close to the trivia which Hunt said would have no place in his improvement over the older magazines. But the unknown writers lend a diversity to the subject matter while maintaining the intellectual level and erudition of the *Reflector*, part of the mind of the times which the magazine portrays.

VI

THE *REFLECTOR* AND ITS HISTORICAL AND LITERARY SIGNIFICANCE

The significance of the *Reflector* lies in its contribution to the history and literature of the early nineteenth century, and these two areas are reciprocal in its pages. Hunt's "chronicle for posterity" was founded in order to add a literary voice to the clamor for parliamentary reform (and, they hoped, to increase the income of the founders), and along with the *Examiner* it has earned for Hunt a minor place in the early reform movement. In the literature of the Romantic period the *Reflector* is esteemed for the essays and poems of Hunt and Lamb and for its part in the development of the familiar essay. In the Prospectus to the *Reflector* Hunt speculated about the interaction of politics and literature in his day, and his magazine, in its short life of fifteen months, contributed significantly to both.

When the Hunts established the *Reflector* in 1810 as a storehouse of articles on politics, the theatre, and fine arts, they had already committed themselves fully to the cause of reform. Their *Examiner* was almost an official organ for the reformists because Hunt's literary taste and intellectual qualities attracted readers who appreciated good writing and the reform principles which he advocated. Hunt could find willing contributors in his circle of friends who, predictably, held the same political views, and some of them were fellow alumni from Christ's Hospital. The Hunts intended that the new magazine would broaden the scope of their readership and extend their political influence and reformist views to an even larger and more influential audience than that of the *Examiner*. That reform was greatly to be desired is unquestionable – its success some twenty years later is proof of its need – but the ministry in 1810 vigorously opposed any change despite strong agitation for a broadening of the franchise and criticism of sinecures, nepotism, and corruption. To Hunt reform meant reform in Parliament, and to him all the abuses of the established government centered in the person of the Prince of Wales, who became Regent at the same time that the first *Reflector* appeared.

Thus politics pervades the *Reflector*, not only in the historical or editorial items but in some of the literary works as well. Since the editor and the editorial policy were the same as for the *Examiner*, the Retrospects are mostly repetition of what had appeared in the weekly paper, but since the *Reflector* articles cover three months or more, they have the advantage of a point of view or perspective denied to the *Examiner*. Hunt could with detachment and objectivity consider events in the light of subsequent developments, and rarely did he render a faulty judgment. The Retrospects are not the chronological listings found in other magazines of the time; their value lies in giving the reader a familiarity with the news events that occupied the Englishman of that day, a verbal picture of the times. They call attention to the hope for better things when the Prince of Wales will become Prince Regent, of the keen disappointment in the continuation of the status quo, of the frustrating war against Napoleon and the mounting national debt, of the faulty political philosophy inherited from Pitt, and of the worsening conditions in the business community. In the best of his political essays in the *Reflector* Hunt summarizes the Prince's recent offenses against good taste and good government and warns that a continuation of his present policies would be destructive of the English character and independence. The essay has a quiet and convincing dignity quite different from the snappish tactics of "The Political Examiner", a cooler evaluation of the Prince than the impatient, disrespectful, and deliberately libelous article which was to bring legal action against him a few months later. His dialogue on the subject of the reformists, in the first issue, repeats much of what he said in the *Examiner* and in a pamphlet published the previous winter and is a significant part of Hunt's contribution to reform in its examination of the specifics of reform. For a man who professed to spend most of his time with his books and his poetry, Hunt had an uncommon grasp of the current scene. And in his ability to translate that scene into literary language, Hunt brought journalism and the essay closer together.

While the political essays by other contributors are now of little interest, they do show the unanimity of thought in the Hunt coterie and continue, in varying degrees of heat and bias, the criticism of the government and the suggestions for reform. Some of the best political satires in the magazine are by authors who chose to remain anonymous, but their warning is clear: England's throne could topple as easily as those on the continent. The unidentified E.B.H. in a short satire "On the Advantages of the Present Age" shows clearly that the "advantages" include a king without common sense, mismanagement in the military establishment, corruption in government, and an increasing national debt. Some of George Dyer's lengthy articles relate to the political and social scene, analyzing England's unwritten Constitution and discussing the claims of the Catholics to religious freedom under the Constitution; he reports also on conditions and abuses that he found in a recent tour of schools, hospitals, and other institutions. The best of Barron Field's varied subjects concern the many lawyers who were connected in some way with literary figures of the Romantic period; his descriptions of the men and their courtroom manner provide first-hand impressions and verbal pictures which animate our knowledge of these once-important and influential men.

Reform appears briefly in some of the purely literary works, such as Lamb's essays on the Gunpowder Plot and on the inconvenience of being hanged, as well as in Hunt's poem, "Politics and Poetics". The several articles in the *Reflector* that are concerned with religion reflect the close relationship of the established church to the government and also Hunt's antipathy for the Methodists. But some of the anonymous contributors are more tolerant in their views, one of them discussing religious persecution in general and another writing against a recent attempt to alter the Act of Toleration.

None of the essays in the *Reflector* brought an indictment from the attorney general; he could accomplish his purpose by charging the editor and publisher of the *Examiner*. But without a doubt the *Reflector* was another gadfly to the government and its propaganda reached an influential intellectual audience, one which could appreciate and respond to a literary medium more readily than to a newspaper. Like the *Examiner*, the *Reflector* did its part in molding public opinion and helping to make reform possible. Unfortunately, the *Reflector* was short-lived and it appeared so early in the reform movement that its impact and influence are overshadowed by the weekly newspaper of which it was a literary adjunct. Hunt's effectiveness as a reformist diminished as time went on; his loss of that intense self-confidence so prominent during the *Reflector* period probably stems from his imprisonment from 1813 to 1815, poor health, and the ever-present financial problems. But in these early days of the reform movement, Hunt made his contribution to reform through the *Examiner* and the *Reflector*.

Lamb's essays have been responsible for much of the recognition given the *Reflector* for its contribution to the literature of the Romantic period, with Hunt's poems and an essay or two taking second place. Lamb not only contributed more items of lasting importance, but his stature and position in literature give greater significance to everything he wrote. But without detracting in any way from the excellence of Lamb's essays in the *Reflector*, we should remember that without Hunt and his literary magazine Lamb might never have written the critical and personal essays which he contributed and the development of the familiar essay might have been halted or at least very different. Hunt's magazine gave Lamb the literary and financial encouragement, the freedom of space and subject matter which permitted his genius to grow. Presumably he needed practice, an apprenticeship, in the traditional personal essay before he could go on to Elia. As Watson says, "It is essential to remember that the *Elia* papers did not burst full grown from the brow of their creator. They are the result of training which started with the century-old tradition."[1]

[1] Watson, p. 80.

The fact that Lamb brought the familiar essay to full fruition and that Hunt never quite reached that stage has obscured Hunt's part in its development. Actually, Hunt's "A Day by the Fire" in the fourth issue takes a long step on the road to the familiar essay and in 1812 was ahead of Lamb on that journey, for Lamb's personal essays of that period were still largely traditional. Why did not Hunt continue on that journey? The answer to this question lies to some extent in the mystery of the creative spirit, but probably the distressing events of 1813-1815 and the diminishing of his egotistical ardor were also destructive of the conditions conducive to the production of something as relaxed as the familiar essay. At any rate, Hunt's influence on the development of the genre was greater than the number of his writings in that form would indicate, and his *Reflector* essay may have shown Lamb the way. George L. Barnett has helped to put Hunt in a perspective that is closer to the truth in writing that "due credit and praise has been slow to come to Hunt, and his influence [in the development of the new essay] is still underestimated".[2]

Up to the *Reflector* period Hunt had done little with the personal essay. He had written essays in the style of the *Connoisseur* in the *Traveller* five years before, but these have not survived, and he published an occasional sketch in the *Examiner*. Until he started the *Reflector* he could not begin writing the many personal essays which were to constitute a large part of his life's work. Hunt acknowledged his indebtedness to the eighteenth century essayists and their influence is apparent in his *Reflector* essays in their traditional forms and devices. Lamb too had to wait for the *Reflector* before he could develop his talent in the personal essay, though he had written one, ten years before. He used most of the traditional devices and forms such as letters to the editor, character sketches, exaggeration, literary allusions, and fictitious signatures. The Lamb humor and whimsicality is present in the essays, and it was to become stronger in the Elia essays, but in 1812 Lamb was still getting practice and setting the foundation for his advance to the familiar essay with its subjectivity, nostalgia, and freedom from the externals of the older style.

[2] Barnett, p. 36.

Of the four personal essays by Hunt in the *Reflector,* three are considerably longer than any of Lamb's, taking full advantage of the freedom of space in his magazine. His essays follow tradition except for their abandonment of anonymity, for the familiar indicator hand appears at the end of each essay and he speaks of himself as Mr. Reflector. But Mr. Reflector is still Mr. Hunt, not a persona created by him as Lamb created a separate persona for each essay. In the essays Lamb is a dramatist; Hunt is not. Most of Hunt's personal essays are didactic in their political or social criticism, their advice regarding overindulgence, and their suggestion that common sense can overcome the world's (and men's) ills.

"A Day by the Fire" foreshadows the familiar essay and, as Watson observes, it is "the best example of the essay in transition".[3] The familiar devices of the traditional essay have been omitted; in this essay Hunt is close to the personal revelation of the familiar essay in his use of the first person pronoun, the intimacy of his own room and fireside, and the sense of cozy comfort which he shares with the reader. He communicates directly, conversationally, and avoids didacticism except in recommending the poems that he quotes. The purpose is pleasure rather than instruction, lightness rather than seriousness. In its subjectivity, its interest in nature, and its sensual pleasure the essay is representative of the Romantic period; in its familiar manner and abandonment of traditional devices it looks toward the familiar essays of the 1820's.

Lamb's nine personal essays in the *Reflector* are traditional in style, and their brevity, charm, and mild humor place them among Lamb's most enjoyable and memorable essays. Most of them are in letter form and are first person narrations of what purport to be personal experiences. At least two can be traced to incidents in Lamb's life. He uses the "character" in conjunction with other material and the signature is usually a Latin word related to the subject of the essay. The personal essays by Lamb in this period contain little that is transitional. He comes close to

[3] Watson, p. 76.

the self-revelatory in the essay on hissing at theatres, perhaps because it relates a traumatic experience; in the others he is a dramatist building figures of the imagination, each essay being something of a dramatic monologue in which Lamb disappears and a persona appears. In the personal essay Lamb transferred some of his dramatic aspirations, in which he failed, to a medium in which he was very successful. A primary difference between the personal essays of Lamb and of Hunt lies in Lamb's use of pathos and wry humor. Hunt may appeal to the mind, but Lamb appeals to the heart. A few years after the *Reflector*, Elia was born. A link between the two is "A Bachelor's Complaint", which became an Elia essay when shorn of its epistolary form; it is likewise a link between Lamb's apprenticeship and his mastery of the familiar essay.

In the first few years following the demise of the *Reflector* neither Lamb nor Hunt altered the personal essay to any appreciable extent. Lamb published three essays in the period and Hunt a great many, but none came very much closer to the familiar essay. In Lamb's "On Christ's Hospital and the Character of the Christ's Hospital Boys" (published in *Gentleman's Magazine* in 1813) the objectivity and impersonality yield briefly, toward the end, to a more personal style, a foreshadowing of the Elia essay on the same subject. For Hunt the *Examiner* had to substitute for the *Reflector* as a literary outlet and his essays were largely traditional in form. After inaugurating his "Round Table" series in 1815 he departed occasionally from the traditional devices, but his personal essays did not develop as Lamb's were to develop in the Elia series, nor did they achieve the place that has been accorded to Lamb's. The Firesider never quite matched Elia.

The best of the critical essays in the *Reflector* are, of course, Lamb's essays on Shakespeare and Hogarth, and they are among his most frequently anthologized works. The continuing respect for the two essays is indicative of Lamb's ability as a writer and his perception as a critic. Hunt's critical writings in the magazine are more in the nature of reviews and are not limited to literary criticism but include all of the major arts except music. His "The

Feast of the Poets" is literary criticism in verse form, and though it is superficial and biased in its original form, it is significant in its revelation of Hunt's immaturity as a literary critic. He was disrespectful to Wordsworth without knowing Wordsworth's poetry; in his attitude toward his contemporaries he was as audacious as he was in his castigation of the Prince Regent. Since Hunt and Lamb were acquainted from the early months of 1811 and Lamb had been a close friend and admirer of Wordsworth for many years, it is surprising that Hunt, who was a voracious reader, could have been unacquainted with Wordsworth's compositions. In the poem Hunt unnecessarily antagonized many people and created much of the ill feeling which resulted in some of the later attacks on him, but its irreverent attitude is characteristic of Hunt of the pre-Surrey Gaol period. The "Feast" was the beginning of his inclination toward literary criticism and a resultant lessening of political criticism, and the two revisions of the poem reflect not only a growing acquaintance with contemporary poets and their work but also a growth in his critical perceptivity, a talent which enabled him to recognize the genius of newcomers like Shelley and Keats.

The critical writings by members of the Hunt coterie are of minor importance but are interesting in the extent to which they reflect Romantic or Wordsworthian principles. They also bring some fleeting notice to those members of the coterie and a realization that they were important men at that time. Dr. John Aikin was the oldest of the contributors, and his eleven contributions show him to be abreast of his times in literary and social thought. His essay comparing Thomson and Cowper as descriptive poets is his best essay in the *Reflector*. In it he concludes that Cowper is the superior poet by citing familiar Romantic principles: common language, close observation of nature, avoiding personifications, and emphasis on imagination and fancy. It was to Aikin, not Lamb, that Hunt pointed with pride when he wrote the little introductory paragraph to the second binding of the magazine late in 1812. Octavius Gilchrist, the grocer-critic and champion of John Clare, is represented by an essay which investigates a possible source for Shakespeare's *Tempest*.

The contributions from Hunt's classmates at Christ's Hospital show them to be helpful and productive but deficient in literary criticism. James Scholefield wrote on poets at college and criticized current methods of teaching classical languages; Thomas Barnes, the future editor of the *Times*, wrote learnedly on the poetry of Propertius. Thomas Mitchell likewise contributed no literary criticism, but helped his friend with items of a miscellaneous nature. In an age which was producing many fine poets, George Dyer asked why there were so few good poets, concluding that true genius and a divine inspiration are lacking in many – the very reasons why Dyer himself was a third-rate poet. The anonymous contributors sent excerpts from recently-published memoirs, criticisms of Hume's popular but inaccurate history of England, and a survey of the current philosophy of education which shows a familiarity with the work and ideas of the Edgeworths.

As promised by the editor in the Prospectus, the fine arts received considerable emphasis in essays by Hunt and his friends. Hunt's purpose was to improve the taste and appreciation of the nation and to share with his readers what he considered the best in literature and art. He had sound judgment in matters concerning the fine arts, and posterity has concurred in his evaluations of such artists as Reynolds, Turner, and West. Hunt's brother Robert is very likely the author of two anonymous articles, one on the engravers Frey and Piranesi, the other on the artist, James Barry. Strangely enough Hunt, who was a fine amateur musician, did not include music under the fine arts in the *Reflector*.

Hunt's *Reflector* provided an outlet for the writings of his coterie, but it was not limited to that group by any means, though that common interest was responsible for much of the homogeneity and cohesiveness of the group. The *Reflector* was responsible for Lamb's inclusion in the coterie. The addition of Lamb and a number of anonymous contributors established a trend which, if the magazine had continued, would have broadened the authorship in the magazine and in time would have made it outgrow the original coterie. The *Reflector*'s fees were an incentive not to be denied, but Hunt's friends were loyal and generous – and prolific – in their contributions.[4]

In the ambiguity of the word *reflector* – a mirror and a thinker – may be found, in essence, the significance of the *Reflector* and a representation of its editor. While Hunt never called his magazine a mirror, he did hold up a mirror to the times, recording external events and, as a typical Romantic, looking toward the internal, the "mind" of the times as expressed by the individual: "The man himself – in his air and attitude – and in the mind that looks out of his general aspect", as he expressed it in the Prospectus. Hunt himself is the thinker implied in the title, reflecting his several roles of political and theatrical critic, poet, translator, and personal essayist. As the sharer of literature and art, Hunt also becomes the reflector which diffuses the light of knowledge.

The *Reflector* was a product of its times as well as a mirror of them, and it also affected the society and literature of its times in a somewhat unobtrusive way. Though overshadowed by the *Examiner* in reform matters, it added a measure of literary force to the movement. It provided the literary and economic incentive for personal essays by Lamb and Hunt and was influential in the development of the familiar essay. It brought Lamb and Hunt together initially, beginning a friendship which was to mean so much to both men. Hunt's own contribution to the growth of the familiar essay is contained in one of his *Reflector* essays, and that essay may have influenced Lamb. The success of the *Reflector* in molding the taste of its subscribers is difficult to assess, but with Hunt's good judgment in esthetic matters, it could only have bettered their appreciation of literature and the fine arts. In its short life the *Reflector* fulfilled the promise that it would be a chronicle for posterity, recording the mind of the times, but it was considerably more. It was an affective journal which contributed its share to political reform and recorded an important step in the growth of the essay and in the literary development of Charles Lamb and Leigh Hunt.

[4] See Appendix II.

APPENDIX I

AUTHORSHIP OF THE *REFLECTOR* ARTICLES

To conserve space, the titles of the *Reflector* articles in the following list have been shortened. When the British Museum copy or a clear signature in the magazine have been the sources, the names of the authors are listed without qualification. When internal evidence has been the basis of identification, the name is placed in parentheses; a question mark indicates that the identification is logical but specific evidence is lacking. A blank space after the title indicates that the author is still unknown.

Volume I, Number 1
(Issued about January 1, 1811)

Article	Prospectus	Hunt
I	The British as a Thinking People	Hunt
II	The Reformers, a Dialogue	(Hunt?)
III	Shakespeare Sermons	Barron Field
IV	Pernicious Effects of Methodism	
V	The Law-Student	Barron Field
VI	On the Claims of Propertius	Thomas Barnes
VII	Stafford's Niobe	Thomas Barnes
VIII	Greek and English Tragedy	(James Scholefield)
IX	Defects in Public Institutions	George Dyer
X	On the English Constitution	George Dyer
XI	Account of a Familiar Spirit	Hunt
XII	The Origin of Shakespeare's *Tempest*	Octavius Gilchrist

XIII	On Early and Late Hours	Barron Field
XIV	Modes of Living and Thinking	John Aikin
XV	Proper Spirit for a Young Artist	Hunt
XVI	The Travels of Reason	Voltaire/Hunt
XVII	On War	John Aikin
XVIII	Dr. Bentley	(James Scholefield)
XIX	Atys the Enthusiast	Hunt
XX	On the Catholic Claims	(George Dyer)
XXI	State of the Arts in England	Hunt
XXII	Retrospect of the Theatre	Hunt
XXIII	Retrospect of Public Affairs	Hunt
XXIV	Short Miscellaneous Pieces:	
	(1) Robert Herrick	Thomas Barnes
	(2) On Charles I	

Volume I, Number 2
(Issued about July 27, 1811)

Article		
I	Church and Constitution	
II	Passages from de Bassompierre	
III	Remarks on Hume's History	
IV	Greek and English Tragedy	(James Scholefield)
V	On the English Constitution	George Dyer
VI	Inquiries Concerning Instinct	(John Aikin?)
VII	On Learning Greek and Latin	George Dyer
VIII	On the Arts and Sciences	George Dyer
IX	Politics and Poetics	Hunt
X	The Pruriencies of Our Old Poets	Barron Field/Hunt
XI	The Law Student	Barron Field
XII	Inconveniences from Being Hanged	Charles Lamb
XIII	On Academies of Art	(Robert Hunt?)
XIV	On Theophrastus	Thomas Barnes
XV	On Personal Deformity	Charles Lamb
XVI	The Gunpowder Treason	Charles Lamb
XVII	Poets at College	(James Scholefield)

XVIII	Retrospect of Public Affairs	Hunt
XIX	The Public Spirit of the Times	Hunt
XX	Retrospect of the Theatre	Hunt
XXI	Short Miscellaneous Pieces:	
	(1) A Libel Discovered	
	(2) A Sketch	Thomas Barnes
	(3) What Constitutes a Madman	Barron Field
	(4) Effects of Wealth	Barron Field
	(5) Ambiguities from Proper Names	Charles Lamb
	(6) The Anapest	

Volume II, Number 3
(Issued October 25, 1811)

Article		
I	Character of the Prince Regent	Hunt
II	On the Act of Toleration	
III	On the Independence of the Judges	(George Dyer)
IV	Dower out of Personality	(Thomas Barnes?)
V	On the English Constitution	George Dyer
VI	Comparison between Thomson and Cowper	John Aikin
VII	Religious Persecution	
VIII	Genius and Character of Hogarth	Charles Lamb
IX	Sensation and Perception	(John Aikin?)
X	The Law Student	Barron Field
XI	On Hissing at the Theatres	Charles Lamb
XII	Greek and English Tragedy	(James Scholefield)
XIII	On Burial Societies	Charles Lamb
XIV	Treatment of Intellectual Disorders	Hunt
XIV(sic)	Advantages of Present Age	
XV	The Proper Objects in Education	
XVI	Retrospect of Public Affairs	Hunt
XVII	Talents of Frey and Piranesi	(Robert Hunt?)

XVIII	Retrospect of the Theatre	Hunt
XIX	Short Miscellaneous Pieces:	
	(1) True Enjoyment of Splendour	Hunt
	(2) On Humour	John Aikin
	(3) On Optimism	John Aikin
	(4) Memoirs of La Noue	
	(5) Re Jack Ketch	(Thomas Mitchell)
	(6) The Patriot's Almanac	(Thomas Moore?)
	(7) Poem	(Thomas Mitchell)
	(8) On the Bodleian Library	George Dyer
	(9) A Pair of Portraits	(Thomas Mitchell)
	(10) "The Balloon" (poem)	Lucy Aikin

Volume II, Number 4
(Issued March 23, 1812)

Article		
I	On the Favourites of Princes	
II	Contempt of Popularity	
III	On the Privileges of a Pedestrian	(John Aikin?)
IV	Defects in Classical Education	(James Scholefield)
V	Professor Porson Vindicated	(James Scholefield)
VI	Letters on Biography	John Aikin
VII	So Few Excellent Poets	George Dyer
VIII	On the English Constitution	George Dyer
IX	On Garrick, and Acting	Charles Lamb
X	The Feast of the Poets	Hunt
XI	Antiquity of the English Language	(Thomas Mitchell)
XII	Letters of Mlle l'Espinasse	(Thomas Mitchell)
XIII	Specimens from Fuller	Charles Lamb
XIII(sic)	A Bachelor's Complaint	Charles Lamb
XIV	On Medical Science	(John Aikin?)
XV	Retrospect of Public Affairs	Hunt
XVI	Making Beaux and Belles Useful	Thomas Barnes
XVII	Change of Structure induced on Animals by Domestication	

XVIII	A Farewell to Tobacco	Charles Lamb
XIX	Edax on Appetite	Charles Lamb
XIX(sic)	Hospita on Immoderate Indulgence	Charles Lamb
XX	A Day by the Fire	Hunt
XXI	Athens and England	
XXII	Retrospect of the Theatre	Hunt
XXIII	The Good Clerk	Charles Lamb
XXIV	Short Miscellaneous Pieces:	
	(1) On Words	
	(2) Latin verse	(Thomas Mitchell)
	(3) Latin verse	Thomas Barnes
	(4) The Devil	Barron Field
	(5) The Exaggerator	Barron Field
	(6) Letter regarding Assessments	John Aikin
	(7) Old Maids	

APPENDIX II

SUMMARY OF THE INDIVIDUAL CONTRIBUTIONS TO THE *REFLECTOR*

Leigh Hunt*	22½ items	230 pages
Charles Lamb	14	93
John Aikin	11	134
Lucy Aikin	1	1
Thomas Barnes	8	50
George Dyer	11	148
Barron Field	9½	51
Octavius Gilchrist	1	8
Thomas Mitchell	6	28
James Scholefield	7	54
Robert Hunt (?)	2	26
Thomas Moore (?)	1	2
Unidentified	18	120
Total	112 items	945 pages

* Not counting the Prospectus, the apology preceding the third issue, or the explanation for discontinuance inserted in the second binding of the *Reflector*.

A SELECTED BIBLIOGRAPHY

Abrams, Meyer Howard, *The Mirror and the Lamp: Romantic Theory and the Classical Tradition* (New York, Oxford University Press, 1953).

Ades, John I., "Charles Lamb, Shakespeare, and Early Nineteenth-Century Theater", *PMLA*, LXXXV (May 1970), 514-526.

Antal, Frederick, *Hogarth and His Place in European Art* (London, Routledge & Kegan Paul, 1962).

Aspinall, A., "The Social Status of Journalists at the Beginning of the Nineteenth Century", *RES*, XXI (July, 1945), 216-232.

The Autobiography of Leigh Hunt, ed. J. E. Morpurgo (London, The Cresset Press, 1949).

Baldwin, Edwin Chauncey, "The Relation of the Seventeenth Century Character to the Periodical Essay", *PMLA*, XIX (1904), 75-114.

Barnet, Sylvan, "Charles Lamb's Contribution to the Theory of Dramatic Illusion", *PMLA*, XLIX (1954), 1150-1159.

Barnett, George L., *Charles Lamb: The Evolution of Elia* (Bloomington, Indiana University Press, 1964).

—, "Charles Lamb's Part in an Edition of Hogarth", *MLQ*, XX, iv (December, 1959), 315-320.

Bate, Walter Jackson, *From Classic to Romantic* (Cambridge, Harvard University Press, 1946).

Bibliography of the Writings of Charles and Mary Lamb: A Literary History, comp. J. C. Thomson (Hull, J. R. Tutin, 1908).

Blunden, Edmund, "Thomas Barnes (1785-1841): Literary Diversions of an Editor", *TLS* (10 May, 1941), p. 226.

—, *Leigh Hunt and His Circle* (New York and London, Harper & Brothers, 1930).

—, *Leigh Hunt's "Examiner" Examined* (New York and London, Harper & Brothers, 1928).

—, *Charles Lamb and His Contemporaries* (Cambridge, The University Press, 1933).

—, *Romantic Poetry and the Fine Arts* (British Academy Lecture, 1942) (Oxford, The University Press, 1942).

Brewer, Luther A., *My Leigh Hunt Library – The Holograph Letters* (Iowa City, Iowa, University of Iowa Press, 1938).

—, *Some Letters from My Leigh Hunt Portfolio* (Cedar Rapids, Iowa, 1929).

Brougham, Henry Peter, *Historical Sketches of Statesmen Who Flourished in the Time of George III*, Second series, 2 vols. (Philadelphia, Lea and Blanchard, 1839).

Bryan, William Frank, *The English Familiar Essay* (Boston, Ginn and Company, 1916).

Clark, Roy Benjamin, *William Gifford, Tory Satirist, Critic, and Editor* (New York, Columbia University Press, 1930).

The Correspondence of Leigh Hunt, ed. Thornton Hunt, 2 vols. (London, Smith, Elder and Company, 1862).

Cunningham, Peter, "Herrick and Southey", *N & Q*, X (First series) (1854), 27.

Diary, Reminiscences, and Correspondence of Henry Crabb Robinson, ed. Thomas Sadler, 2 vols. (Boston, Fields, Osgood & Company, 1869).

The English Dramatic Critics: An Anthology 1660-1932, ed. James Agate (New York, Hill and Wang, n.d.).

English Romantic Poets and Essayists, ed. Lawrence Huston Houtchens and Carolyn Washburn Houtchens (New York, Modern Language Association, 1957).

Erdman, David V., "Blake's 'Nest of Villains' ", *K-SJ*, II (1953), 61-71.

Fogle, Stephen F., "Leigh Hunt and the Laureateship", *Studies in Philology*, LV (October, 1958), 603-615.

—, "Leigh Hunt's Lost Brother and the American Legacy", *K-SJ*, VIII (1959), 95-101.

—, "Skimpole Once More", *NCF*, VII (1952), 1-8.

Fukuda, Tsutomu, *A Study of Charles Lamb's "Essays of Elia"* (Tokyo, The Hokuseido Press, 1964).

Gaunt, William, "On the Genius and Character of Hogarth: 1697-1764: A Bi-centenary Tribute", *The CLS Bulletin*, CLXXX (November, 1964), 465-466.

Graham, Walter, *English Literary Periodicals* (New York, Thomas Nelson and Sons, 1930).

Griswold, Louis, "The Diction of Charles Lamb", *Quarterly Journal of the University of North Dakota* (1927).

Haven, Richard, "The Romantic Art of Charles Lamb", *ELH*, XXX (1963), 137-146.

Henderson, Arnold, "Some Constants of Charles Lamb's Criticism", *Studies in Romanticism*, VII (Winter, 1968), 104-116.

Hine, Reginald Leslie, *Charles Lamb and His Hertfordshire* (London, J. M. Dent & Company, 1949).

The History of the Times: The Thunderer in the Making, 1785-1841 (New York, The MacMillan Company, 1935).

Howe, Will David, *Charles Lamb and His Friends* (New York, Bobbs-Merrill Company, 1944).

Hudson, Derek, *Thomas Barnes of The Times* (Cambridge, The University Press, 1944).

Hunt, Leigh, *Lord Byron and Some of His Contemporaries*, 2 vols. (London, Henry Colburn, 1828).

Leigh Hunt's Autobiography, The Earliest Sketches, ed. Stephen F. Fogle (Gainesville, Florida, The University of Florida Press, 1959).

Leigh Hunt's Dramatic Criticism, ed. Lawrence Huston Houtchens and Carolyn Washburn Houtchens (New York, Columbia University Press, 1949).

Leigh Hunt's Literary Criticism, ed. Lawrence Huston Houtchens and Carolyn Washburn Houtchens (New York, Columbia University Press, 1956).

Johnson, Reginald Brimley, *Christ's Hospital: Recollections of Lamb, Coleridge and Leigh Hunt* (London, G. Allen, 1896).

Keats, Shelley, Byron, Hunt and Their Circles, ed. David Bonnell Green and Edwin Graves Wilson (Lincoln, University of Nebraska Press, 1964).

Kroeber, Karl, *Romantic Narrative Art* (Madison, University of Wisconsin Press, 1960).

Landré, Louis, *Leigh Hunt (1784-1859) Contribution à l'Histoire du Romantism Anglais*, 2 vols. (Paris, Société d'Édition "Les Belles-Lettres", 1936).

——, "Leigh Hunt: His Contribution to English Romanticism", *K-SJ*, VIII (1959), 133-144.

Law, Marie Hamilton, *The English Familiar Essay in the Nineteenth Century* (Philadelphia, University of Pennsylvania, 1934).

The Letters of Charles Lamb, to which are added those of his sister Mary Lamb, ed. E. V. Lucas, 3 vols. (London, J. M. Dent & Sons, Ltd., 1935).

Lowell, Amy, *John Keats* (Boston and New York, Houghton Mifflin Company, 1925).

Lucas, E. V., *At the Shrine of St. Charles* (London, Methuen & Company, Ltd., 1934).

——, *The Life of Charles Lamb*, 2 vols. (New York and London, G. P. Putnam's Sons, 1907).

Marshall, William H., *Byron, Shelley, Hunt, and The Liberal* (Philadelphia, University of Pennsylvania Press, 1960).

Memoirs, Journal, and Correspondence of Thomas Moore, ed. Lord John Russell (London, Longmans, 1856).

Monkhouse, William Cosmo, *Life of Leigh Hunt* (London, Walter Scott, 1893).

Morgan, P. F., "A Note on George Dyer", *The CLS Bulletin*, #136 (May, 1957), 159.

Morley, Frank Vigor, *Lamb Before Elia* (London, J. Capt, 1932).

Patterson, Charles I. Jr., "Charles Lamb, Shakespeare, and the Stage Reconsidered", *Emory University Quarterly*, XX (1964), 101-107.

Political and Occasional Essays of Leigh Hunt, ed. Lawrence Huston Houtchens and Carolyn Washburn Houtchens (New York, Columbia University Press, 1962).

Proctor, Bryan Waller, *An Autobiographical Fragment*, 2 vols. (London, George Bell and Sons, 1877).

——, *Charles Lamb: A Memoir* (Boston, Roberts Bros., 1866).

Ralli, Augustus, *A History of Shakespearian Criticism*, 2 vols. (New York, The Humanities Press, 1949).

Roberts, Michael, "Leigh Hunt's Place in the Reform Movement, 1808-1810", *RES*, XI (January, 1935), 58-65.

Henry Crabb Robinson on Books and Their Writers, ed. Edith J. Morley, 3 vols. (London, J. P. Dent & Sons, Ltd., 1938).

Rollins, Hyder Edward, *The Keats Circle: Letters and Papers, 1816-1878*, 2 vols. (Cambridge, Harvard University Press, 1948).

Shine, Hill, and Helen Chadwick Shine, *The Quarterly Review under Gifford: Identification of Contributors 1809-1824* (Chapel Hill, The University of North Carolina Press, 1949).

Stout, George D., *Political History of Leigh Hunt's Examiner*, Washington University Studies – New Series, Language and Literature, No. 19 (St. Louis, 1949).

Talfourd, Sir Thomas Noon, *Final Memorials of Charles Lamb*, 2 vols. (London, E. Moxon, 1848).

—, *Memoirs of Charles Lamb* (Philadelphia, J. B. Lippincott Company, 1892).

Tibble, John William and Anne Tibble, *John Clare, A Life* (New York, Oxford University Press, 1932).

—, *John Clare: His Life and Poetry* (London, Heinemann, 1956).

Trewin, J. C., "Leigh Hunt as a Dramatic Critic", *Keats-Shelley Memorial Bulletin*, X (1959), 14-19.

Trollope, William, *A History of the Royal Foundation of Christ's Hospital* (London, William Pickering, 1834).

Walton, Clyde C. Jr., "Leigh Hunt: Spirit of an Age", *Amateur Book Collector*, III (October, 1952), 6-7.

Watson, Melvin R., *Magazine Serials and the Essay Tradition, 1746-1820* (Baton Rouge, Louisiana State University Press, 1956).

—, "The *Spectator* Tradition and the Development of the Familiar Essay", *ELH*, XIII (September, 1946), 189-215.

Wheeler, Paul Mowbray, "The Great Quarterlies of the Early Nineteenth Century and Leigh Hunt", *SAQ*, XXIX (July, 1930), 282-303.

Wilson, John Iliff, *The History of Christ's Hospital* (London, J. Nichols and Son, 1821).

Winbolt, Samuel Edward, *The Poetry and Prose of Coleridge, Lamb and Leigh Hunt, selected and edited with a synchronous narration of their lives* (London, W. J. Bryce, 1920).

Woodring, Carl R., "Charles Lamb in the Harvard Library", *Harvard Library Bulletin*, X (1956), 208.

The Works of Charles and Mary Lamb, ed. E. V. Lucas, 7 vols. (London, Methuen & Company, 1903).

Wright, Dudley, "Charles Lamb and George Dyer", *English Review*, XXXIX (1924), 390-397.

—, "Leigh Hunt on Wordsworth and Coleridge", *K-SJ*, VI (1957), 59-73.

INDEX